SpringerBriefs in Economics

More information about this series at http://www.springer.com/series/8876

Ahmad H. Juma'h • Doris Morales-Rodríguez
Antonio Lloréns-Rivera

Labor Markets and Multinational Enterprises in Puerto Rico

Foreign Direct Investment Influences and Sustainable Growth

Springer

Ahmad H. Juma'h
Inter American University of Puerto Rico
San Juan, Puerto Rico

Doris Morales-Rodríguez
Inter American University of Puerto Rico
San Juan, Puerto Rico

Antonio Lloréns-Rivera
Inter American University of Puerto Rico
San Juan, Puerto Rico

ISSN 2191-5504 ISSN 2191-5512 (electronic)
SpringerBriefs in Economics
ISBN 978-3-319-17177-7 ISBN 978-3-319-17178-4 (eBook)
DOI 10.1007/978-3-319-17178-4

Library of Congress Control Number: 2015937419

Springer Cham Heidelberg New York Dordrecht London

Printed on acid-free paper

Springer International Publishing AG Switzerland is part of Springer Science+Business Media (www.springer.com)

Preface

It is striking to see the simultaneous presence of a high rate of unemployment and an educated workforce among the population in Puerto Rico. How has this happened? How can we overcome this economic situation and return to a sustainable path of economic growth in the short and long term? To begin to answer these questions from Academia, we need to conduct economic, objective, and scientific research. This book presents some of the results of various doctoral dissertations conducted in the International and Interregional Business Doctoral Program of the Metropolitan Campus at Inter American University of Puerto Rico. For the Faculty of this doctoral program, this publication presents an objective and scientific contribution on these economic issues which are of great relevance to Puerto Rican society. The databases used were those of the Puerto Rico Industrial Development Company, Puerto Rico Labor Development Administration, Department of Labor and Human Resources, Planning Board, and Department of the Treasury of Puerto Rico; all of whom we wish to thank for the opportunity they provided for the utilization of their databases in an effort to improve the socioeconomic well-being of the residents of Puerto Rico.

Scientific research on economic affairs represents one of the main contributions of the university to society; from the faculty, it is one of the main ways of inserting ideas and alternatives in the public discussion directed to the betterment of social coexistence in Puerto Rico. This implies that we are considering the future of the life of the social and economic fabric that enables individuals to achieve their goals, aspirations, and life expectations.

Doctoral dissertations have a main academic objective for the university and its doctoral students. But this does not end there; economic research also has relevance for society. This book represents an effort to publicly reveal the results of these investigations and propose alternatives of public policy that can direct individual effort towards the achievement of a higher level and better quality of life. It is undeniable that achieving greater economic and social well-being in a geographic area is based on individual productivity that workers and employees can achieve in the different places of work, such as companies and industries. Therefore, the increase in productivity of the economy of Puerto Rico requires the effort of the individual in terms of business and labor. This book expresses the reasons to engage individuals to embark on this productive groundwork and start a journey towards a better future of social and economic life in Puerto Rico.

San Juan, Puerto Rico — Ahmad H. Juma'h
San Juan, Puerto Rico — Doris Morales-Rodríguez
San Juan, Puerto Rico — Antonio Lloréns-Rivera

Acknowledgements

Many colleagues contributed with the investigations and doctoral dissertations that made possible the writing of this book. The authors are grateful to the faculty of the School of Economics at Inter American University of Puerto Rico, Metropolitan Campus, especially to Dr. Felix Cuć, Dr. Ángel Ruiz, Dr. Juan Karman, Dr. Enrique Martínez, Dr. Carlos Rodríguez, Dr. Denis Arroyo, and Dr. Carlos Fonseca. We also want to thank the dean and chair of the School of Economics and Administrative Sciences, Prof. Fredrick Vega and Prof. Myrna Reyes. We would like to express our thanks to Dr. Bernardo Batiz-Lazo for his participation in the book evaluation.

The authors wish to extend their appreciation to the Board of Directors of the INDUNIV Research Consortium for their support to this work, especially to Mr. Iván Lugo and Dr. Carlos Tollinche. We are grateful to the Puerto Rico Manufacturers Association (PRMA) for their collaboration and support of this project, in particular to Mrs. Waleska Rivera, Mr. Rodrigo Masses, and Mr. Boris Jaskille. Finally, we are indebted to the Advisory Board of the Puerto Rico Manufacturers Association comprised of Mr. Bartolomé Gamundi and Mr. Héctor Jiménez Juarbe and especially to Mr. William Riefkohl for his contribution and comments to this document.

Contents

Author Biography

Ahmad H. Juma'h, Ph.D., C.P.A. Prof. Juma'h earned a Ph.D. in Accounting and Finance from Manchester Business School, Manchester University, UK. He obtained a master's degree in Business Administration with majors in Accounting and in Finance, a bachelor's degree in Accounting, and a Bachelor of Science with a major in Mathematics from Inter American University of Puerto Rico. He is a Certified Public Accountant (CPA) and possesses a certificate of higher education in Finance from Baruch College/IAUPR. Juma'h has taught accounting, finance, and strategic management courses in various universities in Puerto Rico since 1987. He has published more than 30 articles in international and professional journals with respect to outsourcing, materiality implications, performance measurements, R&D, FDI, behavioral accounting and finance, and multinationals' activities. Currently, he coordinates the Doctoral Program in Finance (DBAF) in the Economics School in the Faculty of Business Administration of Inter American University of Puerto Rico, Metropolitan Campus.

Doris Morales-Rodríguez, Ph.D. Dr. Morales-Rodríguez holds a doctorate in Entrepreneurial and Management Development in International Business from Inter American University of Puerto Rico, Metropolitan Campus. She earned a master's degree in Labor Relations from Inter American University of Puerto Rico and a bachelor's degree in Social Science with major in Political Science from the University of Puerto Rico. She has conducted research on economic incentives, relocation, transaction costs, financial performance, and competitiveness. She teaches economics and business administration in various universities in Puerto Rico. She has published several articles in academic and professional journals.

Antonio Lloréns-Rivera, Ph.D. Dr. Lloréns-Rivera earned his Ph.D. in Public Policy and Management with majors in Public Finance and Urban Economics from The Ohio State University (OSU) in the United States of America. Also, he obtained a master's degree in Economics and a Bachelor of Social Science degree in Economics from University of Puerto Rico, Río Piedras Campus. He has conducted research on fiscal policies, management, and the labor markets in Puerto Rico. He has taught graduate courses in economics, labor economics, finance, and public finance at Inter American University of Puerto Rico, Metropolitan Campus, since 1996. He has published several articles in academic and professional journals.

Contributors of Specific Chapters

Miriam Basem Hassan-Lombardi, Ph.D. Dr. Basem Hassan-Lombardi (Chapter 3) obtained her doctorate in Entrepreneurial and Management Development in International Business from Inter American University of Puerto Rico, Metropolitan Campus. She obtained a master's degree in Economics and a bachelor's degree in Business Administration with a major in Marketing from University of Puerto Rico. She has conducted research on foreign direct investment, exports, labor force, economic growth, and economic feasibility. She has given lectures on economics and has published in academic and professional journals. She currently serves as a strategic economist at the Puerto Rico Industrial Development Company.

Arlyn Landrau-Febres, Ph.D. Dr. Landrau-Febres (Chapter 5) obtained her doctorate in Entrepreneurial and Management Development in International Business from Inter American University of Puerto Rico, Metropolitan Campus. She holds a master's degree in Industrial Management from Inter American University of Puerto Rico and a Bachelor of Science with a major in Industrial Engineering from University of Puerto Rico, Mayaguez Campus. As part of her professional experience, she has provided advisory services in the areas of Industrial Engineering and Industrial Management to companies in different industrial sectors. She currently serves as an economic feasibility analyst in the Puerto Rico Industrial Development Company. She has conducted research on outsourcing and manufacturing.

Tamara Torres-Morales, Ph.D. Dr. Torres-Morales (Chapter 6) obtained her doctorate in Entrepreneurial and Management Development in International Business from Inter American University of Puerto Rico, Metropolitan Campus. She has a master's degree in Management from Metropolitan University of Puerto Rico and a Bachelor of Science with major in Industrial Chemistry from University of Puerto Rico. She has conducted research on the perception of managers in establishing R&D centers and the pharmaceutical industry. She has taught strategic management, global management, and legal and regulatory management courses. Currently, Dr. Torres-Morales serves as a consultant in Property Management Company of Puerto Rico and is project manager for AMGEN.

Chapter 1
Introduction

Puerto Rico's economy was transformed from the agricultural base to a manufacturing base by strategy plan known as Operation Bootstrap or in Spanish "Manos a la Obra". The Industrial Incentives Act[1] applicable to Puerto Rico helped to establish businesses through tax exemptions on income and property for a period of 10 years, marking the era of industrialization.

Operation Bootstrap in the 1950s was the reason for the experienced economic growth in Puerto Rico. That industrialization was based mainly on tax exemptions to attract a massive influx of American capital and entrepreneurs in the manufacturing sector (Alameda and González 2001). The increase in gross domestic production per capita was remarkable (from $328 in 1950 to $ 27,451 in 2012).[2] The growth in the labor force during the golden era of industrialization (1950–1970) also was evident. The economic development on the Island can be classified into four stages: 1947–1965: Labor intensive; 1966–1976: Capital intensive promotion of petrochemical; 1977–1992: High-technology; 1993 to present: The Search for New Model of Economic Development (Alameda and González 2001).

However, the Island faces similar economic problems as other countries since 2008. It is notable that the level of unemployment has increased significantly and the level of labor participation is declining. Among the factors that have contributed to the detriment of the economic situation are transfers or relocation of manufacturing operations located in Puerto Rico to other countries, which have increased in recent years. This raise not only cause the loss of jobs in the primary industry sector but also contributes to the decrease of competitiveness of the Island as location for foreign direct investment, and brings the urgency of developing a new approach to economic development strategy.

---

[1] 188 Act of May 11, 1942, as amended known the Puerto Rico Industrial Development Company Law.

[2] Data of Planning Board of Puerto Rico.

A.H. Juma'h et al., *Labor Markets and Multinational Enterprises in Puerto Rico*, SpringerBriefs in Economics, DOI 10.1007/978-3-319-17178-4_1

Foreign Direct Investment

Investment patterns of multinational companies are increasingly complex (OECD 2008). Countries compete aggressively for new investments and achieve higher levels of efficiency and productivity. Foreign direct investment (FDI) is of great importance for development and economic growth of countries. FDI is associated with the markets openness, technology transfer, job creation and increases in productivity and efficiency, among other factors (Gondor and Nistor 2012; Rodríguez and Bustillo 2010).

FDI comprises two typical assets: capital and technology or a number of intangible benefits. Therefore, it is more likely that FDI is important in industries with significant specific business assets, intangibles, based on knowledge. Most FDI occurs through the establishment of multinational companies in different countries. The term corresponds to a multinational company with assets or employees in more than one country (Guillen 2002). Multinationals have great power in the global economy. More than 50,000 companies worldwide can be classified as such and have subsidiaries under its control worldwide. It is estimated that 85 % of companies with FDI are located in developed countries of Western Europe, Spain, USA, Canada, Australia and Japan and in emerging countries, such as South Korea, Taiwan, Mexico, Argentina and Brazil.

Economic Incentives

The Government of Puerto Rico has historically sought to encourage the establishment of manufacturing companies in the Island. The vast majority of the established companies are American in their origin. However, many of the companies that have settled in Puerto Rico are classified as a multinational.

The strategy of Economic Development of Puerto Rico has focused on attracting US capital using the law of industrial incentives. Since 1976, the federal government granted a tax exemption by the Section and/or Article 936 of the US Internal Revenue Code on company profits generated in Puerto Rico. Section 936 allowed US corporations in Puerto Rico to repatriate their profits with no tax obligation. That law also exempts the income from the investment of federal corporate tax, on condition that three quarters of the total profits came from trade or manufacture, and that they are reinvested in Puerto Rico (Dietz 2001; Laboy and Toledo 2006; Bram et al. 2008).

Section 936 and the law of industrial incentives influenced that manufacturing becomes the main productive sector of Puerto Rico. Manufacturing companies have contributed about 46 % of GDP and over 95 % of exports of Puerto Rico since 1980. The benefits under Section 936 were repealed in 1996 and ended in 2006 with a grace period granted by Section 30-A.

In Puerto Rico, there were several different laws to promote economic development, among which is the present Economic Incentives for the Development of Puerto Rico (73 Act of May 28, 2008). This responds to strategic public policy decisions on Puerto Rico. The law aims to: (1) provide the business environment and the right to continue developing economic opportunities to local industries, (2) offer an attractive tax proposal to FDI and keep up with the most competitive jurisdictions of high-tech industries and high added value, (3) ensure a link between industries and government promoted from Puerto Rico and all its members, which is based on public transparency, stability, certainty and credibility, (4) support initiatives from the private sector, academia, community businesses, and municipalities, leading to economic development of Puerto Rico through innovation, research and development, and investment in infrastructure for a better quality of life and efficient industrial operations, (5) reduce high operating costs and streamline regulatory constraints that discourage the competitive position of Puerto Rico, (6) to reduce energy costs through the different alternatives of renewable sources, and (7) recognize the importance of decentralization of government and, according to the above, support the efforts that are being developed at regional level to promote economic development and technological innovation (73 Act 2008).

Economic incentives from the Government of Puerto Rico for the promotion and retention (special incentives to establish industries, incentives special fund for economic development and tax exemptions) are subject to manufacturing job creation. Each of the incentives granted considering the commitment of jobs generated by companies, either because it is newly created or they will be expanding their operations. Similarly, it seeks jobs retention through personnel training to face technological change and regulatory compliance. In addition, the retention of jobs is intended through rescue or recovery operations of a company and/or to strengthen and modernize operations (MO-INC-001 Norms for Incentive Management, PRIDCO 2006; MO-DNE-002 Norms for the Administration of Special Fund for Economic Development, PRIDCO 2009).

Similarly, the law is set to join the government and educational institutions, known as the Act to Create the Trust for Science, Technology and Research of Puerto Rico (214 Act. of August 18, 2004). It seeks to accelerate the implementation of initiatives in science, technology and research and stimulate the development of new markets, attracting investors and the proliferation of new jobs (214 Act 2004). It is the major law of incentives for the establishment and development of research and development of the manufacturing industry in Puerto Rico.

Research and Development

The activity of research and development (R&D) is important for the prosperity and competitiveness of a country. The prevailing view is that private investment in R&D produces a social benefit. The same is not limited to scientific research in a lab, includes a lot of elements for a new product, the development of new processes, evolution and continuous improvement. Overall R&D comprises creative work on a systematic basis in order to increase the stock of knowledge, including knowledge of man, culture and society and the use of this reserve to devise new applications (Ernest and Young 2010).

An innovation is the introduction of a new or improved product (good or service), a process, a new marketing method or a new organizational method in the internal practices of the company, organization of the workplace or external relations. Innovation processes differ greatly from sector to sector both in terms of development, rate of technological progress, links and access to knowledge, and in terms of organizational structures and institutional factors. In high technology sectors, R&D plays a central role in innovation activities, while other sectors rely to a greater extent in the adoption of knowledge and technology.

The types of R&D can be classified into four categories: (1) products, materials, or processes of adaptation or improvement, (2) basic research materials or products, (3) R&D rationalized the search for efficiency foreign production, and (4) strategic asset search for R&D, aiming monitor or gain technological competitive advantages (Dunning and Narula 1995).

In Puerto Rico, the R&D is promoted by economic incentives which include a super deduction of up to 200 % of expenditures. In addition, the Trust for Science, Technology and Research of Puerto Rico, created by the government, organizations are nonprofit and Pharmaceutical Industry and Academia Research Consortium (INDUNIV) to develop innovation initiatives. Despite these efforts to establish R&D centers as well as the generation of patents are in a high degree of lag relative to other countries. The positioning of Puerto Rico in the era of knowledge economy and the development of the Island as a location for innovation axis could prove essential to boost the economy by attracting FDI and creating jobs.

Subcontracting and Value Chain

FDI that allows the execution of subcontracting is a strategic decision that affects the organizational structure of companies that perform this type of transaction, reason behind the analysis and evaluation of the various factors that could impact on operating results expected and benefits of market position that you want to achieve. Outsourcing through FDI is expected to generate economic activity that is beneficial to both the company making the investment and to the country receiving it. Outsourcing abroad (offshoring) and FDI is more frequent in capital-intensive industries located in countries with more relative scarcity of capital (Yeaple 2006). The outsourcing of manufacturing or services also may be an indicator that the company will be making a relocation of its activities as a strategy in the pursuit of competitiveness.

Puerto Rico still needs to formulate an economic development strategy that fits the new global landscape. The strategy set by the Operation Bootstrap project proved successful until the late 1970s, but was design for a totally different global order. The Island has not been able to establish a long-term strategy that gives way to a real transition to as stage of development in the era of knowledge and technology. It is necessary to articulate a development strategy to mobilize the economy. It should concentrate its resources and efforts in areas that actually still have opportunities as the manufacture of generic drugs and outsource non-core activities to other countries. Also, it needs to focus on and increase efforts to attract R&D. The new strategy needs to consider factors such as: restructuring of the education and integration of industry and academia, labor market flexibility, competitiveness of energy sector, restructuring and greater integration of government institutions and streamlining bureaucratic processes to establish business on the Island. In forming this strategy, governmental, private and community sectors need to contemplate devolvement models of countries that resemble Puerto Rico and who have demonstrated superior economic index, such as Singapore and Ireland. But the most important is to raise awareness about the need to make changes in the way of life, and the individual role as a productive entity in Puerto Rico.

Chapter 2
Structural Change in the Employment of Puerto Rico

Employment is a key factor in the economic growth of countries. By this, a more equitable social development and more efficient production system are promoted. At present, global employment is affected by challenges generated by economic crisis of higher proportions and requirements of higher production efficiency in multinational enterprises, which are the main determinants of the globalized world.

In Puerto Rico, employment and the labor market has specific characteristics that add to the ones existing worldwide. The economy of the Island is characterized by high unemployment and low levels of labor force participation. The labor market is increasingly reduced and the economy reflects inability to create jobs. In this chapter the development of the labor market and employment is showing and structural change in employment in Puerto Rico.

Industrial Development and Employment in Puerto Rico

During 1950s, the 36 % of employment in Puerto Rico was generated by the agricultural sector. This industry also contributed to the 18.2 % of gross domestic product (Ruiz 2006). In the 1960s employment in agriculture began moving down on the benefit of the growing manufacturing sector. The share of agriculture contributed to employment change from 36 % in 1950 to 22.8 % in 1960 to 9.9 % in 1970 (Irizarry-Mora 2000). Currently accounts for 2 % of employment and contributes less than 1 % to the GDP of the Island.

Given the process of industrialization by invitation economic development of Puerto Rico has focused on manufacturing for export to the US market. This in turn, represented the first structural change in the economy and employment in Puerto Rico. For the 1970s the manufacturing sector was the main generator of jobs, followed by the commercial sector. The manufacturing sector reached its peak in job creation in the 1990s, and has since begun to decline (see Table 2.1).

A.H. Juma'h et al., *Labor Markets and Multinational Enterprises in Puerto Rico*,
SpringerBriefs in Economics, DOI 10.1007/978-3-319-17178-4_2

Table 2.1 Employments in the industrial sectors: agriculture, manufacturing, trade and services: 1950–2010 (in thousands)

Decade	Agriculture	Manufacturing	Trade	Services	Government
1950	210	111	92	81	47
1960	131	91	98	78	64
1970	66	132	130	117	107
1980	41	141	141	136	185
1990	35	166	190	213	218
2000	22	162	243	304	252
2010	17	99	242	335	252

Source: Data obtained from Historical Series Employment and Unemployment Department of Labor and Human Resources of Puerto Rico

From mid-1970s, manufacturing began to reflect a downward trend in job creation in relation to the growing trend reflected in the jobs generated by the commercial and services sectors (see Table 2.1). For the 1980s, manufacturing contributed directly to 19 % of employment in the 1990s with 17 % and already, in the early 2000 contributed to 11 % of employment in the Island (Toledo 2009). In the mid-1980s, a new structural change arises as a result of industrial reorganization that arises in the Puerto Rico's economy after the recession of the early 1980s, promoting an increasing trend of employment in industrial sectors manufacturing, trade and services (Toledo 2009).

However, capacity to create jobs in the manufacturing continues to decline relative to participation in direct employment in the economy and the annual growth rate (Ruiz 2006, 2007). Since 1995, the manufacturing sector reduced its growth trend for changes associated with the elimination of Section 936 (Toledo 2009). Paradoxically, since its introduction in 1976, Section 936 was already affecting the growth rate of employment in the manufacturing sector because it led to a bias for high productivity industries, but little effect on employment (Martínez et al. 2004; Irizarry-Mora 2000; Toledo 2009).

Since the mid-1990s to the present, a downward trend in employment generated by manufacturing remains constant. This signals a new structural change of employment in Puerto Rico. This change has the services sector as the main creator of jobs, contributing 33 % of employment in 2012, compared to 9.2 % of employment provided by the manufacturing industry for the same year. However, manufacturing accounted for 46 % of GDP and 99 % of exports in 2012, remaining as the primary productive sector in the Island.

Labor Market in Puerto Rico

In decades of Puerto Rico's emerging economy, in 1950–1970, average unemployment rate of 12.8 % was maintained. However, these numbers increased to the point that by 1983 unemployment rates of 23.5 % was reported. Since the 1990s, the unemployment rate has decreased but still remains in figures close 10 % (Martínez et al. 2004; Toledo 2009). This shows that Puerto Rico has not yet managed to lower the unemployment rate to single digit figures. Unemployment is an indicator of the degree of utilization of human resources in the economy (Alameda 2000). However, other labor market indicators are important to analyze the degree of growth and development of the economy.

The labor force (working group) is measured considering all individuals who have the legal age and the minimum requirements to be included in the economically active population in the categories of employees and/or unemployed (ILO 2012). In Puerto Rico the labor force includes all persons aged 16 or more who are able to work and are not institutionalized, that is held in prisons, hospitals for chronic illnesses, nursing homes and serving in the armed forces (DLHR 2010). The labor participation rate represents the proportion of the labor force that actively participates in the labor market (ILO 2012). Both indicators reflect the size and the degree of labor market activity in the economy.

Since the beginning of the era of industrialization in 1950, the workforce of Puerto Rico has reflected an upward trend (see Table 2.2). However, this trend has begun to show changes. Official data from the Bureau of Statistics, Department of Labor and Human Resources of Puerto Rico show that since 2008 there is a tendency of contraction in the labor force is presented, and that it has been maintained for 2014 (see Fig. 2.1). Also, it is important to consider that the growing tendency of the civilian non-institutional population has begun to show signs of contraction in 2012. This may imply that the Puerto Rico's labor market is shrinking.

With the initial boom of American capital in the Island's manufacturing and the displacement of the workforce into the industry, the labor participation rate increased two percent, from 52.6 % in 1947 to 54.6 % in 1950. Since then the labor participation rate has reached its highest levels of participation during the 1970s in 1971 with a 48.4 % share, and in the 1990s in 1997 with 48.1 %. However, the labor force participation rate has maintained a downward trend averaging 44 % from 2004 to 2014 (see Fig. 2.2).

Table 2.2 Labor market in Puerto Rico (1950–2000) (in thousands)

Decade	Population	Labor force	Participation rate	Active workers	Unemployment	Unemployment rate	Out of working group
1950	1,289	704	54.6	601	103	14.7	585
1960	1,396	635	45.5	558	77	12.1	760
1970	1,607	771	48	668	83	10.7	836
1980	2,116	916	43.3	760	156	17.1	1,200
1990	2,495	1,132	45.4	972	161	14.2	1,363
2000	2,806	1,203	46.1	1,162	131	10.1	1,513

Source: Historical Series Employment, Unemployment and Worker Group Natural Year Average 1947–1969 and Historical Series Employment and Unemployment Natural Year Average 1970–2010, Bureau of Labor Statistics, Department of Labor and Human Resources of Puerto Rico

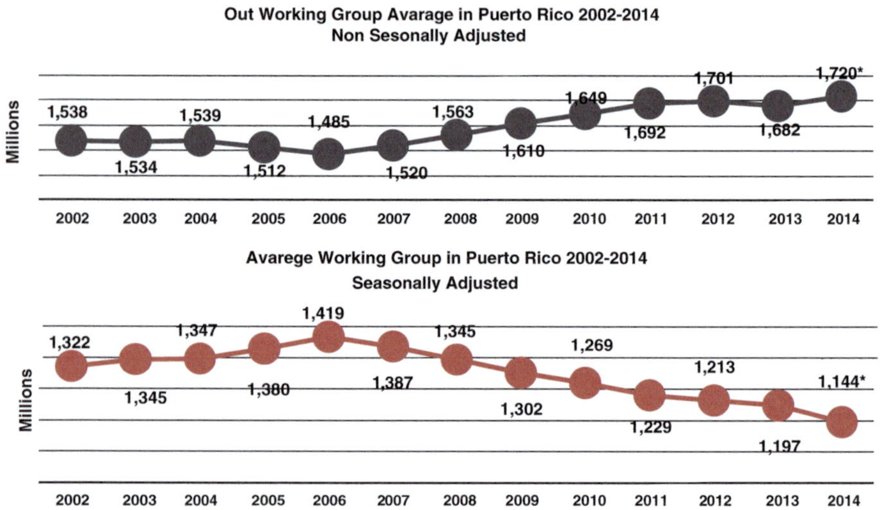

Fig. 2.1 Statistics on Working Group and out of Working Group in Puerto Rico (2002–2014). *Source*: Historical Series Employment and Unemployment Average Natural Year 1970–2010; Employment and Unemployment in Puerto Rico Publication, Bureau of Labor Statistics, Department of Labor and Human Resources of Puerto Rico. (*Asterisk*) The year 2014 presents statistics until November 2014

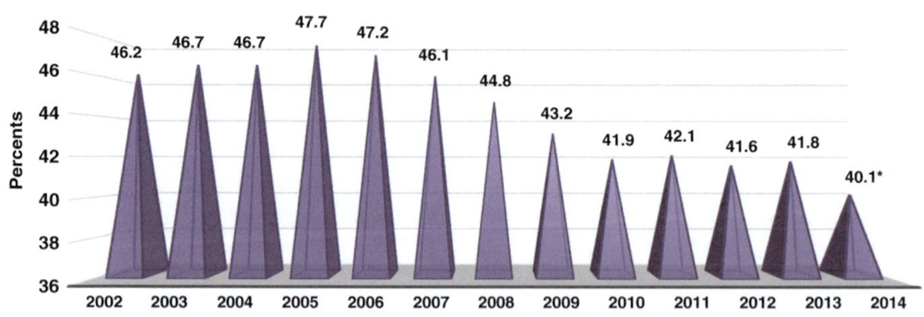

Fig. 2.2 Labor participation rate in Puerto Rico (2002–2014). *Source*: Historical Series Employment and Unemployment Average Natural Year 1970–2010; Employment and Unemployment in Puerto Rico Publication, Bureau of Labor Statistics, Department of Labor and Human Resources of Puerto Rico. (*Asterisk*) The year 2014 presents statistics until November 2014

The low labor force participation has been attributed to several factors such as; underemployment or part-time, high rate of dependency of families that receive welfare support through transfers from the US Federal Government due to the poverty of Puerto Rico in relation to the income of the United States. The people received about $ 15,176.7 million for 2013, with benefits such as Nutritional Assistance Program, TANF, Pell Grants and Medicare among others (see Table 2.3). Also, the informal or underground economy uses a portion of the active population (Aponte 2005; FED New York 2012; Kliksberg and Rivera 2007). Individuals who

Table 2.3 Net disbursements of Federal Government as percentage of GNP to Puerto Rico (current prices for fiscal years 2006 & 2013)

	Fiscal year in $ million		Growth annual
Net disbursements (in thousands)	2006	2013	average rate %
Transfer payments	$9,725.9	$15,176.7	6.6 %
Contributions to public sector	$2,418.5	$3,773.2	6.5 %
Net expenditure of the operation of federal agencies	$1,114.0	$1,704.3	6.2 %
Customs duties	$9.6	$0.0	–
Taxes on shipments	$346.3	$245.9	−4.8 %
Total	$13,614.3	$20,894.1	6.3 %
Puerto Rico payments to the Federal Government	$3,687.8	$3,542.4	−0.6 %
Total net disbursements	$9,926.5	$17,351.7	8.3 %
GNP at current prices	$57,854.3	$70,740.3	2.9 %
Percent	17.1 %	24.5 %	7.4 % points

Source: Adapted from the "La contabilidad macroeconómica de la dependencia" by Santos Negrón Díaz in Sin comillas, December 18, 2014. http://sicomillas.com. Data from the Statistical Appendices of Governor Economic Report, 2013

choose to avail this type of welfare assistance from the federal government have weighed between this alternative and a minimum wage job (in Puerto Rico is $7.25 per hour worked), without any benefit or small marginal benefits; also, this job opportunity can be part-time. It should be noted that, according to the US Census Bureau, 45 % of the population is classified as living under the poverty level, so they qualify for aid.

While other countries and states in the United States have higher welfare assistance than the residents of Puerto Rico, they present a higher labor participation rate. The orientation of social dependence of the people of Puerto Rico has been generated by a political system that is subject to a colonial relationship with the United States. Moreover, this could explain part of the relationship between welfare assistance and the low level of labor participation in Puerto Rico (Blanco-Peck 1992).

In 2014, official statistics from the Department of Labor and Human Resources of Puerto Rico (Worker Survey Group) established that the civilian non-institutional population of Puerto Rico was made up of 2,870,000 individuals (see Fig. 2.3), and estimated the labor force at 1,144,000 (see Fig. 2.1). Also, a labor participation rate of 40.1 % was estimated (see Fig. 2.2). It establishes employment at 983,000 individuals and/or positions of occupied employment (see Fig. 2.4). It also notes a population of 1.720 million persons outside the group (see Fig. 2.1). Compared to 2013, these figures indicate that the employed sector continues to decline, showing 30,000 less job in one year (see Fig. 2.4), and an increase of 38,000 individuals outside the labor force (see Fig. 2.1). While reflecting a decrease of 24,000 unemployed persons (see Fig. 2.4), the unemployment was 1.4 % less than in 2013 for a 14 % unemployment rate (see Fig. 2.5). For 2014, a reduction in labor rate of 1.7 % is observed (see Fig. 2.2).

Reduction in the civilian non-institutional population and the labor force can be caused by increased emigration of the population. The changes that occur in the

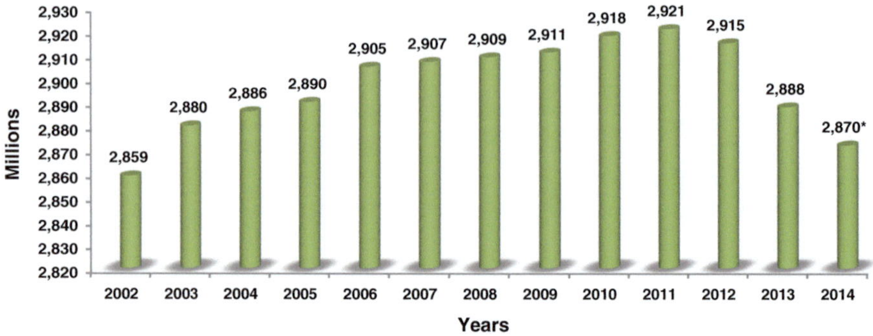

Fig. 2.3 Statistics no-institutional for civilian population in Puerto Rico (2002–2014). *Source*: Historical Series Employment and Unemployment Average Natural Year 1970–2010; Employment and Unemployment in Puerto Rico Publication, Bureau of Labor Statistics, Department of Labor and Human Resources of Puerto Rico. (*Asterisk*) The year 2014 presents statistics until November 2014

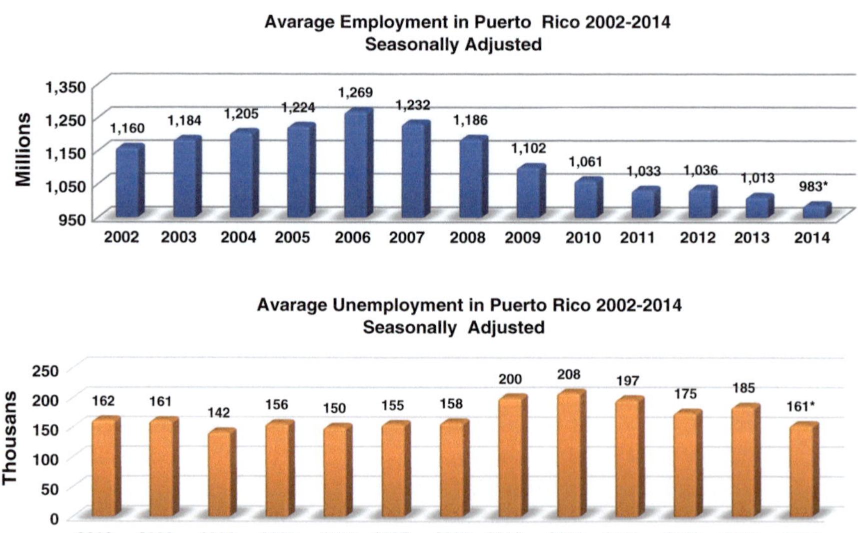

Fig. 2.4 Average of employment and unemployment in Puerto Rico (2002–2014). *Source*: Historical Series Employment and Unemployment Average Natural Year 1970–2010; Employment and Unemployment in Puerto Rico Publication, Bureau of Labor Statistics, Department of Labor and Human Resources of Puerto Rico. (*Asterisk*) The year 2014 presents statistics until November 2014

migratory flow can affect the demographic distribution of the population and labor market, causing a further reduction in the stock of human capital (Pol 2004). Puerto Rico's population has declined by nearly 300,000 in the last decade, from 3.8 million in the year 2000 to3.5 million for 2012 as reflected in the revised Census Bureau

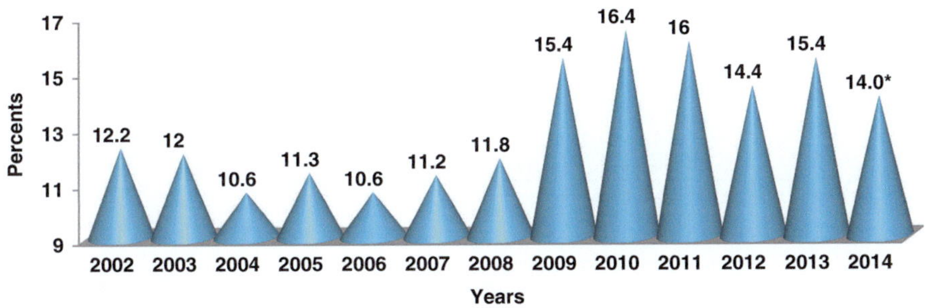

Fig. 2.5 Unemployment rate in Puerto Rico (2002–2013) (Seasonally Adjusted). *Source*: Historical Series Employment and Unemployment Average Natural Year 1970–2010; Employment and Unemployment in Puerto Rico Publication, Bureau of Labor Statistics, Department of Labor and Human Resources of Puerto Rico. (*Asterisk*) The year 2014 presents statistics until November 2014

data (Marxuach 2012; Villamil 2012). This migration possibly reflects increased probability of employment, the wage differential and free labor mobility to the United States (Pol 2004).

In addition to this migration, another factor to consider is the aging of the population, to 22 % of which is composed by persons 62 years or older. This further reduce the workforce. Despite the marked emigration, employment rate in Puerto Rico for 2012 was estimated at 35 %, the lowest in the Western Hemisphere (Silva-Huyke 2013), the trend is continue decreasing in 2014 and estimated at 34.2 %. This demonstrates the inability of the economy to create jobs.

Changes of the Employment in Puerto Rico

The globalization of markets and the elimination of tax benefits of Section 936 have brought changes in the employment sector in Puerto Rico (Toledo 2009). These changes in employment are characterized by the way in which jobs are created and destroyed. According Toledo (2009), for the period 1991–1995, the average rate of total job creation was 3.6 % and decreased to 1.7 % for the period 2001–2007. Moreover, from 1991 to 1995, jobs were lost at a rate of 1.3 % annually, increasing in the period 2001–2007 to 2.07 %. This loss of jobs has contributed to the sharp economic slowdown (Rodríguez 2008), which from 2008 is compounded with the crisis in the global economy.

In the manufacturing, the average rate of job gains fell from 2.7 % during 1991–1995 to 1.2 % in 2001. While in the trade and services sectors, the average was 4.5 % in the period 1991–1995 and 1.95 % in the period 2001–2007. In addition, the manufacturing sector in the period 2001–2007 reflected an increase in job losses of 2.16–4.3 % (Toledo 2009). Table 2.4 shows that from 1990 to 2013, employment in manufacturing has declined nominally about 50 %.

Table 2.4 Non-agricultural employment wages for manufacturing companies in Puerto Rico: 1990–2013 (seasonally adjusted, in thousands)

Year	January	February	March	April	May	June	July	August	September	October	November	December	Mean	Mean fiscal year
1990	159.3	161.4	161.3	160.9	159.6	158.7	158.3	157.8	157.1	158.0	156.5	155.6	158.7	N/A
1991	154.5	154.6	153.4	152.6	152.8	152.7	153.5	153.6	154.4	154.0	154.6	154.7	153.8	155.3
1992	154.5	154.2	154.9	154.9	154.7	154.7	154.1	154.1	154.1	154.8	154.8	155.1	154.6	154.4
1993	155.7	155.4	155.5	155.8	156.3	155.9	156.5	157.1	156.7	152.8	153.4	154.1	155.4	155.1
1994	154.3	154.9	154.4	155.5	155.3	156.0	155.0	155.8	156.2	156.8	156.7	157.1	155.7	155.1
1995	159.1	159.6	159.7	158.6	158.8	158.6	159.3	158.7	158.4	158.7	159.0	159.2	159.0	157.7
1996	160.4	157.4	156.2	158.1	158.4	157.7	156.7	157.9	155.4	157.1	158.0	157.0	157.5	158.5
1997	155.2	155.5	156.1	156.2	154.9	155.6	154.6	154.1	154.5	154.1	153.1	151.6	154.6	156.3
1998	150.5	150.7	150.0	148.7	148.2	147.4	147.8	147.5	146.8	144.0	145.7	144.7	147.7	151.5
1999	145.6	144.3	143.2	146.9	146.7	145.8	145.3	144.5	143.5	141.0	141.8	141.2	144.2	145.8
2000	143.7	143.8	142.3	143.0	143.2	142.5	143.0	142.5	142.3	142.5	142.2	141.3	142.7	143.0
2001	138.7	138.3	137.6	136.1	135.2	135.1	130.1	128.2	127.5	126.1	124.9	124.1	131.8	139.6
2002	123.1	121.9	121.3	122.6	123.7	122.9	120.0	120.7	120.2	118.9	118.5	118.8	121.1	124.7
2003	117.8	118.2	118.4	118.1	117.5	117.4	117.1	117.7	118.0	119.2	119.6	118.9	118.2	118.7
2004	119.1	119.0	118.6	118.3	118.2	118.1	118.0	118.5	118.1	117.9	117.9	118.2	118.3	118.5
2005	117.9	117.4	117.1	116.3	115.7	115.4	114.7	113.4	113.5	114.1	114.2	114.5	115.4	117.4
2006	112.2	111.9	111.5	110.7	110.7	110.0	109.5	109.0	108.2	108.1	107.8	107.3	109.7	112.6
2007	107.6	107.6	107.0	107.2	107.3	107.5	107.4	106.4	105.8	105.2	104.8	104.1	106.5	107.8
2008	103.5	103.0	102.8	102.5	102.1	101.2	101.1	100.2	99.8	98.8	98.1	98.7	101.0	104.1
2009	96.9	95.4	93.9	93.4	92.3	91.6	90.8	90.1	89.4	89.0	88.4	88.2	91.6	96.7
2010	88.7	87.9	87.3	86.9	86.7	86.6	86.4	86.3	86.3	86.7	86.1	85.7	86.8	88.3
2011	85.6	85.3	85.3	85.2	84.9	83.9	84.1	84.0	83.6	83.1	82.7	82.6	84.2	85.6
2012	84.6	84.1	84.0	83.2	82.8	82.6	81.4	81.2	80.7	79.7	78.4	77.1	81.7	83.5
2013	75.5	76.3	75.3	75.2	74.5	74.6	74.4	74.3	74.6	75.6	76.3	77	75.3	77.5

Source: Department of Labor and Human Resources Bureau of Labor Statistics Employment Statistics Division. The data are jobs in the manufacturing sector and from the survey of establishments that considers only employees on the payroll of establishments and includes military employees civilly.

The rates listed of job creation and destruction point to a reallocation of labor input across sectors of the economy (Toledo 2009). Therefore, a structural change in employment in Puerto Rico has taken place. In part, this relocation of labor could be related to a difference in productivity among employment sectors which is higher in manufacturing relative to trade and services (Ruiz 2006).

It is also important to consider how the establishment manufacturing plants and/ or retention of plants (companies) promoted by the PRIDCO has affected employment in Puerto Rico. About 2,000 of these plants closed operations from 1978 to 2012. Some closed operations due to the relocation of its activities to other geographical areas that are more profitable. This relocation imply which a loss of competitiveness in the economy of Puerto Rico so that it fails to retain and attract industries in the manufacturing sector. Others companies simply have not been able to respond to changes in the global economy and to increasing operating costs at the local level, so sometimes had to exit the market or make reorganizations. As a result, in all these cases, a loss of jobs occurs (Morales et al. 2012; Laboy and Toledo 2006). Other factors that may contribute to the lack of jobs are the application of the minimum wage, a mismatch between the type of work requirements and human capital; and a hostile business environment for commercial and industrial development, especially regarding the permits process and registration of property process (FED New York 2012).

Conclusions

Reducing the labor market is partly due to the migration of the population seeking employment opportunities, better wages and living conditions. Since 2008, the labor market in Puerto Rico has been shrinking. This situation coincides which the current recession affecting the economy of the Island. At the same time, there is a reduction of labor force and increase in the non-working group. This means that a portion of the workforce has abandoned searching for jobs either because of lack or jobs that do not meet individual expectations of regarding compensation. Also, labor participation rates seem to be affected by federal transfers and welfare assistance to the population. These transfers make dependency more attractive, reducing the insertion of the individuals into the workforce.

Employment in Puerto Rico has been reduced almost in all sectors, but to a greater extent in the manufacturing. It has been noted a continuous reduction of employment in the manufacturing and proportionally greater in the service sector. This may indicate a structural change in employment in Puerto Rico related to the inter-sectors linkages between manufacturing and services, not necessarily a structural change in the economy itself given the fact that manufacturing remains the main driver of GDP and exports. Moreover, growth in employment in the service sector and trade could respond to changes in consumer demand generated by an increase in income and in propensity to consume. This in turn would explain the current downturn in various industries due to the economic crisis.

Although the structural change in employment could respond to these factors (inter-sector linkages, changes in labor demand and consumption and the propensity to consume), it is clear that the availability of jobs in the manufacturing sector, in turn, is has been affected by the loss of competitiveness of Puerto Rico to retain and attract new manufacturing plants so that the jobs created are maintained and new jobs are created or jobs are replaced in this sector. Several factors have influenced this loss of competitiveness in the manufacturing sector, among them: the elimination of tax benefits of Section 936, the rise in the federal minimum wage that applies in Puerto Rico, various labor regulations and environmental and burdensome process for obtaining permits to establish businesses. This makes it imperative to deepen knowledge about these factors that could deepen the reduction in manufacturing employment and further affect economic development of Puerto Rico.

Chapter 3
Labor Market of Puerto Rico and FDI, Exports and GDP

Section 936 attracted many manufacturing companies in Puerto Rico; in particular, pharmaceutical that prompted the use of high technology. However, its contribution to economic growth and job creation has been questioned. This chapter seeks to identify and compare the relationship between inflows of foreign direct investment (IFDI), exports (EX), Gross Domestic Product (GDP), unemployment rate (UR) and labor participation rate (LPR) of Puerto Rico. For comparison purposes, two jurisdictions were considered: Singapore and Ireland, both of which directly reflected high levels of economic growth and foreign direct investment (FDI).

Comparison of GDP, FDI, EX, UR, and LPR Between Puerto Rico, Singapore and Ireland (1980–2010)

In the mid-1970s and mid-1990s under Section 936, strategies for industrial development in Puerto Rico focused on high-tech manufacturing. The main objectives of these strategies were attracting foreign capital and export promotion in the industrial sectors of pharmaceutical, professional and scientific instruments and electrical machinery. These sectors generate spent most of exports and an increasing proportion of jobs (Aponte 1999; Dietz 2003; Martínez et al. 2004; Collins et al. 2006).

The government instruments to attract investment to the Island, such as local tax exemptions and rent industrial space at favorable costs have not changed since 1976. When comparing the Island jurisdictions such as Singapore and Ireland whose growth strategies and economic development are similar to those of Puerto Rico were not achieved the same results in terms of: increases in GDP, EX and

The chapter is mainly derived from a dissertation conducted by Dr. Basem Hassan-Lombardi (2012), and other works realized by Basem Hassan-Lombardi et al. (2012) and Basem Hassan-Lombardi and Juma'h (2014).

A.H. Juma'h et al., *Labor Markets and Multinational Enterprises in Puerto Rico*, SpringerBriefs in Economics, DOI 10.1007/978-3-319-17178-4_3

IFDI. In turn, has not been able to reduce the unemployment rate to single digits and increase labor participation rate at least 50 % (Dietz 2003; Martínez et al. 2004). Table 3.1 presents the comparison of data per decade between 1980 and 2010.

In the 1980s Puerto Rico's GDP was higher than that of Singapore and IFDI was higher than Ireland. In the 1980s to compare variables GDP, IFDI and EX can be seen that there is no significant difference between the three countries. Back in the 1990s Singapore flags surpass those of Puerto Rico and Ireland in almost all cases except Ireland's GDP which remains the highest with $ 48.167 million.

In the 1990s, characterized by the liberalization of markets, the movement of capital flows between nations and emphasis on globalization, both Ireland and Singapore reflect a higher than Puerto Rico economic growth. The same applies to the level of exports of both countries. In 2000 and 2010 all economic variables analyzed were more favorable for Singapore and Ireland.

One of the reasons why Puerto Rico reflects slower economic growth over the past two decades is that IFDI was much lower than the amounts received by Ireland and Singapore during those years. Similarly, other factors and variables (political stability, freedom to trade and public policy, among others), which may have adversely affected the economic growth of Puerto Rico and its ability to conduct business.

Vector Autoregressive Model

In the analysis presented in this chapter, vector autoregressive models (VAR) were used to perform the decomposition of variance, which was conducted in five periods. It is identified and compared the interrelationship between inflows of foreign direct investment (IFDI), exports (EX), Gross Domestic Product (GDP) unemployment rate (UR) and labor participation rate (LPR) to Puerto Rico, Singapore and Ireland. Furthermore, the similarities and differences of the interrelationship of variables between the three islands are presented. To analyze and compare the interrelationship of variables the medium term, which is defined over a period of 3 years, was used. By considering the same variables and methodology, this chapter extends the works of Basem Hassan-Lombardi et al. (2012) and Basem Hassan-Lombardi and Juma'h (2014) that considered different term period for the analysis.

The historical series of IFDI, EX, GDP and LPR for Puerto Rico are derived from the Planning Board of Puerto Rico. The data IFDI the EX and GDP are measured in millions of dollars at current prices. The time series of UR obtained from the Bureau of Labor Statistics of the Department of Labor of the United States. Puerto Rico data obtained in fiscal years and include the period from 1980 to 2010.

The historical series data for Singapore and Ireland obtained from UNCTAD databases STAT (2012) of the United Nations. The data IFDI the EX and GDP are measured in millions of dollars at current prices. The time series of the UR were obtained from the databases of "World Economic Outlook" (2011) of the International Monetary Fund. Data were collected in calendar years and include the

Table 3.1 GDP, IFDI EX, UR AND LPR of Puerto Rico, Singapore and Ireland (1980–2010)

	Puerto Rico					Singapore					Ireland				
Year	GDP	IFDI	EX	UR	LPR	GDP	IFDI	EX	UR	LPR	GDP	IFDI	EX	UR	LPR
1980	14,436	657	7,013	17.0	43.3	12,046	1,236	19,375	5.8		21,435	286	8,398	7.3	
1990	30,604	2,138	19,305	14.3	45.5	38,835	5,575	52,730	1.8	69.1	48,167	622	23,747	12.9	60.1
2000	61,702	4,772	38,466	11.0	46.2	94,308	16,484	137,804	2.7	71.0	97,525	25,779	77,222	4.3	67.5
2010	96,261	5,043	61,657	16.0	42.5	222,699	38,638	351,867	2.2		206,600	26,330	116,384	13.6	

Source: Planning Board of Puerto Rico, 2011, U.S. Department of Labor, 2011; United Nations, 2011, International Monetary Fund, 2011. Data for Puerto Rico are presented for fiscal year and for Singapore and Ireland is presented for natural year

GDP, IFDI and EX are measured in millions of dollars at a current prices period from 1980 to 2010. The LPR for Singapore and Ireland includes the period 1985–2006.

In all three cases it was verified whether the time series are stationary or not testing Augmented Dickey Fuller (ADF) performed with trend and intercept. It was also verified the cointegration between the variables using the methodology of Johansen and Juselius (1990). When non-stationary time series and cointegration are identified among the variables, we proceed to estimate the VAR model restricted to term error correction (VEC).

The results of the test were generated in five periods and used to explain the interrelation between the variables in the medium term. To determine the appropriate lag order, the criterion of Akaike (AIC) and Schwarts (SC) were used (Akaike 1974, 1981; Sims 1980; Pindyck and Rubinfeld 1991; Rodríguez 2002, 2004; Chang 2006, 2007; Pfaff 2008; Aktar and Ozturk 2009; Guajarati and Porter 2009).

Relationship Between the Labor Market and the Inflow of Foreign Direct Investment in Puerto Rico, Singapore and Ireland

In the case of Puerto Rico and Singapore and to examine the level of variables, almost all were not stationary, except EX of Puerto Rico and IFDI of Singapore. In the case of Ireland to examine the level of the variables, we found that IFDI, EX and UR are not stationary. Table 3.2 presents the results of testing Augmented Dickey Fuller (ADF).

In all cases (Puerto Rico, Singapore and Ireland) the trace test and the maximum root ((λmax)) were applied to check for cointegration between the time series. In the three islands four cointegrated equations, significant at 1 and 5 % are identified. This result indicates long-run equilibrium between variables and historical series compactly move through time. Table 3.3 includes the results of the cointegration tests.

After verifying that the majority of the time series are not stationary and long-term equilibrium exists between them the restricted VAR model in first differences with the vector error correction (VEC) was estimated. The model was left behind in a period. Based on this model the variance decomposition of Puerto Rico and Singapore was generated. In the case of Ireland was not possible to estimate the VEC, being the country with less data, therefore it is estimated an unrestricted VAR which the variance decomposition for the country was generated. The results were generated in a period of 5 years for the three islands and comparative analysis concentrated in the third period defined as medium term. Table 3.4 presents the results of the variance decomposition.

The results suggest a relationship between the labor market and IFDI in the case of Puerto Rico and Singapore. It was found that the unemployment rate and the rate of labor participation of Puerto Rico and Singapore explained 9 % or more of the IFDI. In the case of Ireland the variable that best explained the IFDI was the GDP

Table 3.2 Augmented Dickey Fuller Test (ADF) of Puerto Rico, Singapore and Ireland

	Puerto Rico					Singapore					Ireland				
t-Statistic	IFDI	EX	GDP	UR	LPR	IFDI	EX	GDP	UR	LPR	IFDI	EX	GDP	UR	LPR
Variables level	−0.40	−3.38***	1.23	−2.43	−0.98	−4.04**	−2.04	−2.15	−2.07	−1.56	−2.49	0.16	−3.59**	−1.78	−3.49***
First differences	−4.37*	−4.52*	−1.89	−3.38***	−4.01**	−5.53*	−4.35*	−3.68**	−6.65*	−3.06	−2.36	−4.95*	−3.47***	−2.67	−1.00
Second differences	−3.44***	−6.53*	−10.22*	−3.48***	−6.71*	−4.38**	−5.64*	−5.24*	−5.74*	−3.91**	0.19	−4.94*	−7.10*	−4.64*	−2.17

ADF realized using tendencies and intercepts. All variables are transformed using natural logarithms
*Significant at 1 %, **significant at 5 % and ***significant at 10 %

Table 3.3 Cointegration Tests of Puerto Rico, Singapore and Ireland

Hypothesis		Puerto Rico			Singapore			Ireland		
H_0	H_1	Eigen value	Trace test	λ_{max} test	Eigen value	Trace test	λ_{max} test	Eigen value	Trace test	λ_{max} test
r=0	r≥1	0.94	195.26*	75.10*	1.00	257.88*	176.57*	0.98	186.57*	69.25*
r≤1	r≥2	0.90	120.16*	62.17*	0.88	81.30*	34.23*	0.95	117.32*	52.52*
r≤2	r≥3	0.74	57.99*	36.63*	0.85	47.07*	30.02*	0.91	64.81*	40.31*
r≤3	r≥4	0.52	21.36*	19.95*	0.63	17.05**	15.78**	0.72	24.50*	21.91*
r≤4	r≥5	0.05	1.41	1.41	0.08	1.27	1.27	0.14	2.58	2.58

Notes: *Significance at 1 % level and **significance at 5 % level, and r indicates the number of cointegrating vectors

The optimal lag in the cointegrating test was selected by minimizing the Akaike information criterion

with 7 %. When analyzing exports, it can be seen that the UR explained 14 % or more of the variables in the three islands. In turn, in the case of Puerto Rico and Singapore IFDI affects exports in 19 % or more, finding that shows a relationship between the variables.

In the three islands IFDI and EX are the variables that best explain the behavior of the GDP. The IFDI explained above 7 % and EX explain over 12 % of GDP in the three cases. In turn, the variables representing the labor market, i.e. the UR and the LPR, explained the behavior of GDP in less than 6 % in all three cases. Both Singapore and Ireland GDP explained over 48 % of UR. In Puerto Rico and Ireland the IFDI explained over 12 % of its UR.

The labor force participation rate (LPR), has similar economic structures by comparing IFDI, EX, GDP and UR in the cases of Puerto Rico and Ireland. In both cases the IFDI explained about 27 % of the LPR and 8 % level EX. In turn, in Puerto Rico and Ireland GDP explained about 5 % of their LPR and UR explained about 9 % of the LPR in both cases. In the case of Singapore, analyzing the LPR, economic structure resembles the other two islands in terms of EX and UR.

Conclusions

The analysis shows the relationship between IFDI, EX, GDP and the labor market in Puerto Rico, Singapore and Ireland. The economic structures of the three islands, in terms of the variables under study are similar. In all three cases cointegration between the time series was found, implying that there is long-term equilibrium between the variables. In the case of Puerto Rico, seeking to emulate the patterns of development and economic growth of Singapore and Ireland are expected to consecutive increases in IFDI and the level of EX, could reduce the unemployment rate and increase the interest of Puerto Ricans to join the workforce. Such changes could generate increased economic growth and improvements in income levels and quality of life of Puerto Ricans.

Table 3.4 Percentage of composition of variance analysis in the medium-term of Puerto Rico, Singapore, and Ireland

Puerto Rico					Singapore					Ireland				
IFDI					**IFDI**					**IFDI**				
IFDI	*EX*	*GDP*	*UR*	*LPR*	*IFDI*	*EX*	*GDP*	*UR*	*LPR*	*IFDI*	*EX*	*GDP*	*UR*	*LPR*
74.36	2.96	2.66	9.82	10.20	56.63	9.23	3.87	8.90	21.37	85.58	4.34	6.88	0.62	2.58
EX					**EX**					**EX**				
IFDI	*EX*	*GDP*	*UR*	*LPR*	*IFDI*	*EX*	*GDP*	*UR*	*LPR*	*IFDI*	*EX*	*GDP*	*UR*	*LPR*
18.57	56.11	3.17	18.75	3.39	23.84	50.58	8.60	14.12	2.85	2.41	75.77	1.99	15.05	4.79
GDP					**GDP**					**GDP**				
IFDI	*EX*	*GDP*	*UR*	*LPR*	*IFDI*	*EX*	*GDP*	*UR*	*LPR*	*IFDI*	*EX*	*GDP*	*UR*	*LPR*
12.35	16.24	65.10	4.74	1.58	16.27	66.41	13.81	2.52	0.98	6.65	12.28	73.38	1.23	6.46
UR					**UR**					**UR**				
IFDI	*EX*	*GDP*	*UR*	*LPR*	*IFDI*	*EX*	*GDP*	*UR*	*LPR*	*IFDI*	*EX*	*GDP*	*UR*	*LPR*
16.54	3.51	1.79	58.01	20.15	0.06	19.30	48.33	26.04	6.27	12.04	8.81	49.81	28.10	1.24
LPR					**LPR**					**LPR**				
IFDI	*EX*	*GDP*	*UR*	*LPR*	*IFDI*	*EX*	*GDP*	*UR*	*LPR*	*IFDI*	*EX*	*GDP*	*UR*	*LPR*
27.43	7.63	5.01	8.63	51.29	1.12	3.65	28.15	8.96	58.12	34.33	7.67	9.37	9.72	38.91

Cholesky order: IFDI EX GDP UR LPR, all variables are transformed by natural logarithm

The model of economic growth of Puerto Rico, based on attracting FDI, seems appropriate. However, to reduce UR and increase LPR is necessary to diversify and innovate on policies that are used to attract FDI to Puerto Rico. According to the findings discussed it is recommended that development strategies and economic growth that have used other jurisdictions such as Singapore and Ireland to boost their economies.

Key strategies that involve the interplay of the variables considered, is the diversification of exports in terms of products and services and diversification of partners. Although it should be noted that trade diversification is limited according to the political-economic relationship of Puerto Rico and the United States.[1] Puerto Rico needs to anticipate and prepare to face the political and economic changes that may occur both locally and internationally. This minimizes risk and avoids negative abrupt changes in their economic environment. It is necessary to re-evaluate and competitive public policy that is used to promote the attraction of FDI flows to Puerto Rico.

[1] Federal law and US policies governing international relations, migration, customs and national security, regulate communications, labor market, monetary and banking system in Puerto Rico; and links the economy of the Island and the United States under Federal Relations Act of Puerto Rico, also known as the Jones Act (ECLA/CEPAL, 2004).

Chapter 4
Economic Incentives and Determinants to Attract FDI

The globalization increased the fragmentation of production as a result of economies of scale and challenged countries to seek competitiveness with respect to the attraction and retention of multinational companies. As discussed in the first chapter, industrial incentives policies to attract FDI in the manufacturing sector have been essential element in the strategy for the economic development of Puerto Rico from the decade of 1940–1950. The main objective of the chapter is to discuss the current strategy of economic incentives and competitiveness of Puerto Rico in the attraction and retention of multinational companies, with reference to the companies that made closures and relocations in the period 2005–2012.

Industrial Incentives in Puerto Rico

The package of industrial incentives promoted by the Puerto Rico Industrial Development Company (PRIDCO) under 188 Act of May11, 1942 (Industrial Incentives Act)[1] is considered as a favorable factor that contributed to the manufacturing proliferation. Currently, and in the disappearance of the tax benefits of Section 936 and rising cost of labor factor, the strategy of economic development of Puerto Rico has focused to pursuit competitiveness in manufacturing inter alia on economic incentives established in 73 Act. of May 28, 2008, known as Economic Incentives for the Development of Puerto Rico. However, official statistics of the

[1]This law focuses primarily on state capitalism, so the Puerto Rico Industrial Development Company was commissioned to establish state companies for the production of cardboard boxes, bottles, cement and other products. The owner was Government of Puerto Rico. This model will soon reflect its flaws, and in 1947 a new law (346 Act of May12, 1947), which is responsible for provide incentives to private companies settle in Puerto Rico is approved. The state enterprises were sold to private sector (e.g., Ponce Cement).

A.H. Juma'h et al., *Labor Markets and Multinational Enterprises in Puerto Rico*, SpringerBriefs in Economics, DOI 10.1007/978-3-319-17178-4_4

Bureau of Labor Statistics and the Unit for Displaced Workers and Employers to the Workforce Development Administration, Department of Labor and Human Resources of Puerto Rico, show that employment in the manufacturing sector continues to shrink.

Puerto Rico promotes the establishment of manufacturing industries through a promotional strategy by PRIDCO, which is based in the Industrial Incentives Program. This Program includes management and marketing of 104 industrial parks and/or 1,597 owned buildings of the Government of Puerto Rico. The incentives include the lease of buildings to enterprises at a cheaper cost than the private market; and the granting of special incentives to establish industries in which are: the strategic importance project incentive, creation and/or retention of jobs incentive (Basic and Location), cash incentives for the creation or retention of jobs and infrastructure, marketing special incentive, shipping special incentive, training incentive, equipment special incentive, quality control incentive, incentive for industries in Vieques and Culebra, qualification special incentive, certification special incentive and income special incentive. Similarly, based on the granting of financial incentives under 73 Act. of May 28, 2008 (i.e. Law on Economic Incentives for Economic Development of Puerto Rico), which establishes the granting of tax exemption incentives and establishes the Economic Development Special Fund in order to meet the permanence and stability of existing companies (73 Act 2008). The granting of these incentives is part of the strategy for attracting FDI and promotes competitiveness in the global market.

The Office of Industrial Tax Exemption of Puerto Rico (OITE) administers the granting of economic incentives for tax exemption under the decrees established by 73 Act. These incentives have tax exemption benefits such as exemption from property tax for a period uniform 15 years of 90 % for real and personal property, a self-imposed optional for the appraisal of real property that has not been assessed. Total exemption from state excise and IVU in the raw material to be used in the manufacture of finished, machinery, equipment and accessories that are exclusively used in the manufacturing process, building or to comply with environmental regulations products and/or health and safety equipment needed to install in business dedicated call centers, machinery, equipment, spare parts, used in experimental laboratories accessories, fuel used in cogeneration of electricity for own use or affiliates, and as chemical materials for wastewater treatment equipment and efficient energy use. The exemption of municipal license resulting in a 60 % exemption in ordinary cases, 75 % exemption for SME and 90 % exemption for companies established in Vieques and/or Culebra. As the granting of tax credits for the purchase of products manufactured in Puerto Rico, job creation, technology transfer, investment in strategic projects, reduction in energy costs. Moreover, as an incentive rate overall income tax 4 and 12 % on royalties etc. (73 Act 2008).

The Operation Closures and Economic Incentives

During the period 2005–2012, a total of 20,157 job layoffs in manufacturing companies with a workforce of 100 employees or more were reflected.[2] This due to total or partial closures of operations for 13 different reasons (economic, restructuring, relocation, loss of contract, termination of production, low demand, competitiveness, sales agreement, consolidation, eviction of building, staff excess, production cutting and reducing sales). During the period 2005–2012, 75 % of the plants that had partial or total closures for various reasons have been promoted by PRIDCO. A promotion includes the entire process of attraction for the establishment of an enterprise and is considered from the guidance provided on various aspects, market studies, feasibility and permissions. Promotion may also include the granting of economic incentives (industrial incentives and incentives for tax exemption and/or special fund).

The 49 % of plants with partial or total closures were located in buildings rented from the Government of Puerto Rico, a benefit that belongs to the package of industrial incentives offered to promote economic development[3]. Meanwhile special incentives to establish industries granted by PRIDCO to these firms reporting closures or layoffs during the period 2005–2012 amounted to $153,249,363.96, and were awarded in 15 categories (see Table 4.1).

In plants promoted by PRIDCO, 32 % have some type of special incentives to establish industries and 68 % did not reflect record for such incentives. These plants that demonstrated record of special incentives to establish industries, 62 % had operations after the announcement of the closure of some of their plants or layoff (which is considered a partial closure) and 38 % fully closed operations. Special incentives to establish industries were mostly granted infrastructure, special incentives and importance of the project. However, the incentives represent a major outlay of money by the Government of Puerto Rico were granted to stimulate the area of science and technology (see Table 4.1).

Data from the Office of Industrial Tax Exemption of Puerto Rico reflected that from the manufacturing plants that showed closure of operations for various reasons during the period 2005–2012, 83 % of the plants had some tax exemptions granted by law decree, of which 50.5 % continued operations, 48.5 % closed operations, and

[2] These data are from a selected sample of official statistic on labor displacement for various reasons, including relocation; reported by provisions of Worker Adjustment and Retraining Notification Act (WARN) of August 4, 1988 (29 U.S.C. 2101et seq). This law provides that all employers with 100 employees or more has the obligation to report in cases of massive layoffs and closures with a minimum of 60 days prior to departure. This information is compiled since 2005 by the Displacement Workers and Employers Unit, Workforce Development Administration, Department of Labor and Human Resources of Puerto Rico.

[3] The 47 % of plants with partial and/or total closures localized in company's private buildings and 4 % in buildings belonging in part to the companies and part of the Government of Puerto Rico.

Table 4.1 Types of special incentives for industries granted by PRIDCO (2005–2012)

Type of incentive	Number of plants with incentive	Number of incentives granted	Total incentives granted ($)
Training	1	1	2,700
Science and technology	5	6	41,587,510.96
Quality control	1	1	20,000
Special fund	2	2	5,776,000
Importance of project	16	21	13,366,100
Special incentives	12	21	17,038,430
Special incentive ron	1	4	10,280,000
Infrastructure	18	39	26,208,394
R&D	1	1	500,000
Location	8	14	2,773,842
PRIIF (PR incentive investment fund)[a]	5	6	35,262,500
Rescue	1	1	49,000
Tightening	1	1	18,000
Wage subsidy	1	1	209,200
Culebra transportation	1	3	157,687
Total	41[b]	122	153,249,363.96

Source: Data obtained from Record of Economic Incentives for Promotion from PRIDCO
[a]From fund generated revenue of Section 936
[b]Total number of plants with history Special Incentives for Establishing Industries is 41, but, some companies received various incentives and/or the same incentive on more than one occasion

1.5 % remained with distribution centers. The exemptions were granted by the decrees of five different laws that originate from the year 1963 to the year 2008.

Meanwhile, 31 % of plants with the closure of operations for various reasons have reflected both economic incentives (special incentives to establish industries and tax exemption). This represents that from the plants showed record of special incentives to establish industries, 97 % had tax exemption. Also, 61 % of these plants that had both economic incentives continued operations and 39 % closed operations completely. The vast majority of plants with a record of economic incentives were located in buildings owned by PRIDCO.

Relocation of Operation and Economic Incentives of Puerto Rico

A major cause of work shift in the manufacturing sector, it was represented by relocation and a total of 5,714 displaced employees, representing 28 % of the displacement in this sector. The year 2007 had the highest number of operations relocation, resulting in a total of 2,061 displaced. The labor movement of relocation indicates an inefficient strategy of Puerto Rico to retain companies that decide to move their operations to offshore locations that are more profitable.

The countries that are major competitors of Puerto Rico in relation to the relocation of manufacturing operations are firstly, Mexico that counts about 16 % of the total relocation. Second, and in the same proportion of operations transferring were located in Dominican Republic, China, Malaysia and Singapore reaching 6 % for each. Similarly, countries that are listed as competition from Puerto Rico in the shift of manufacturing operations: Germany and Canada (where the operation of a company in each country was allocated), Brazil, Italy and Asian countries (countries where they are intended part of the production when the operation was moved to several locations at once). The pharmaceutical sector is one with more relocation and the electronics sector ranks second.

The 67 % of the plants had relocation of operations was promoted by PRIDCO. Of those plants relocation 48 % localized in buildings with title to the PRIDCO. The 37 % of the plants were operating relocation record showed special incentives to establish industries, of which 52 % maintained operations after announced the closure and/or layoff (which is considered a partial closure) and 48 % fully closed operations. In plants with relocations, 19 special incentives to establish industries totaled $70,788,922. The 19 incentives granted for infrastructure were (4 incentives), special incentives (3 incentives), importance of the project (5 incentives) were granted, P.R. Incentive Investment Fund[4] (4 incentives), location (2 incentive) and science and technology (1 incentive). The 89 % of the plants with relocation have incentives granted tax exemption. From these plants with tax exemption 50 % remained operating and 50 % fully closed operations. In addition, 37 % of plants with relocation reflected record for both economic incentives (special incentives to establish industries and tax exemption). Of these, 60 % remained operating and 40 % closed operations.

There is a relative equity in companies with economic incentives that once kept announced the relocation and to cease operations completely. This implies that economic incentives are an indifferent element to maintain operations in Puerto Rico and/or are not attractive compared to the rest of the world. The assumptions underlying the strategy for economic development of the Island appear to be insufficient competitive in retaining and attracting manufacturing companies.

Economic Incentives Policies of Puerto Rico in Comparison with Competitor Countries in Manufacturing Relocation

When comparing policies of economic incentives of Puerto Rico with its competitors reflected the policies of economic incentives for attracting and retaining manufacturing companies are established in countries like Mexico, Singapore and

[4] Funds from revenue generated from Section 936.

Malaysia agreed to a strategic approach based directed in the development of industries. Singapore and Malaysia are based on promoting the establishment of high-tech industries and the development of innovation. Mexico is particularly based on the promotion of consumer goods industries. Meanwhile, in Dominican Republic incentive policies are based on the establishment and the promotion of Export Processing Zones (Free Zones).

Economic incentives established in the incentive policies of Mexico and Dominican Republic, Puerto Rico's main competitors in relation to relocation of manufacturing operations: electronic, consumer goods and or intensive manufactures that use labor factor are generally minor term that economic incentives established in Puerto Rico. However, Mexico focuses its promotion policies in addition to its appeal in the cost of labor, in its territorial proximity to the United States that allows a distribution channel and a carry for probably cheaper land and agreements of North American Free Trade Agreement (NAFTA). Similarly, the World Economic Forum (2012) has highlighted the advantage that represents the breadth and depth of the Mexican market for FDI as a factor that contributes to its competitiveness. Meanwhile Dominican Republic, strengthening its competitiveness in wages cost of labor with a focus on promoting the Free Zones as a distribution center for exports and tax exemptions they offer strategy.

Moreover, the incentive policies of Singapore and Malaysia compared with those of Puerto Rico have a very different competitive landscape. Both countries offer competitive tax rates in some similar to those of Puerto Rico cases, and others that are much more competitive, particularly in the areas of innovation and technology, where 100 % tax exemption and benefits offered in deductions more broader than in Puerto Rico. The economic stimulus packages of both countries are complemented by a multimodal transport infrastructure appears to be a decisive competitive factor.

Comparing the management and development of buildings and/or industrial parks as an element that is part of the policy of Puerto Rico industrial incentives, it is necessary to establish that in Mexico, Singapore and Malaysia less government intervention is reflected in this type of activity. For example, the Government of Mexico does not develop industrial parks; its work is aimed at regulating the construction industry and to promote it by multinationals. On the other hand, Singapore and Malaysia to promote foreign investment in construction of buildings through its incentive policies, develops industrial parks which are not operated or marketed by the government, that aspect is delegated to the private sector through management companies.

Determinants for Attracting and Retaining FDI

The decision to relocation operations is related primarily to the level of intensity of production factors (labor intensive or intensive in capital/technology factor). From these and the benefits this country in relation to them, will result in varying degrees in a better position to compete. The cost of labor is a key in the decision to relocate

Table 4.2 Average basic wages for labor in manufacturing for working day, Puerto Rico and major competitors in the relocation of manufacturing firms

Country	Average basic wage for labor in manufacturing/day ($)
Malaysia	28.55
Mexico	4.10
Puerto Rico	100.72
Dominican Republic	13.84
Singapore	73.60

Source: Puerto Rico data obtained from Covered Employment and Wages Report Calendar Year, Bureau of Statistics, Department of Labor and Human Resources of Puerto Rico; Mexico data obtained from www.maquilareference.com; Dominican Republic data obtained from National Statistics Office from www.one.gob.do; Malaysia data obtained from Malaysia Investment Development Authority web page (MIDA) www.mida.gob.my; Singapore data obtained from Report of Wage in Singapore, 2011 to the Ministry of Singapore Workforce www.mom.gov.sg

those intensive manufacturing operations in this factor. Thus, Mexico and Dominican Republic appear to outstrip to Puerto Rico those companies intensive in labor factor, as well as Singapore and Malaysia in industries that are technology intensive. In summary, the four main competitors of Puerto Rico in the relocation of manufacturing operations have increased competitiveness with respect to the cost of labor (see Table 4.2). Labor in Puerto Rico has been classified as more skilled than the competition representing countries in the Americas (Mexico and Dominican Republic). The cost of labor is an important factor that companies consider in maintaining or relocate an operation. Similarly, labor regulations in Puerto Rico are more stringent than those of countries that are presented as competitors, which affect the higher cost of labor.

Regarding the technology factor, strategies for economic development in both Singapore and Malaysia are intended to lead the high-tech manufacturing sector and become the main centers of research, development and innovation in the world. Both countries offer competitive tax rates that are similar to those of Puerto Rico, in much broader benefits deductions and better support in the value chain.

The energy issue is another factor that can currently be considered when establishing or move an operation to a country. Regarding this aspect Malaysia appears to be the most competitive in energy cost, ranging between 0.05 and 0.14 cents per kwh industrial rate. It is also important to note that Malaysia has three producer-suppliers of energy, which increases competition and affects the price. Meanwhile, although Singapore has comprehensive policies for the promotion and renewable energy generation appears to be comparable to those of Puerto Rico energy costs, as its rate fluctuates about 0.27 cents.

In addition, a decisive competitive factor Singapore and Malaysia is a significant multimodal transport infrastructure. Both countries have significant maritime transshipment ports. The port of transshipment in Singapore ranks third in the world in its category and transports 50 % of global oil demand. For its part Malaysia has seven sea transshipment ports, one of them ranked among the top 20 ports worldwide. Also have multiple airports. Malaysia in turn has a rail system that connects to the border of Singapore and offers the advantage of serving for transporting raw materials and equipment.

Conclusions

The economic incentives offered by the Government of Puerto Rico are not sufficient to retain the operations of multinational companies, since they lose appeal against the advantages offered in Singapore and Malaysia. The economic incentives that are part of the strategy for economic development may be an element combination, and together with other factors contribute to retain business operations in Puerto Rico, but these by themselves are not sufficient and independent for holding companies. Moreover, they are not an item to Puerto Rico's competitiveness relative to its main competitors in manufacturing high technology and knowledge development.

This requires a reformulation of policies issued economic incentives on the Island, since the tax benefits of current policy established by 73 Act. (May 28, 2008) do not appear to be competitive, especially in established as tax exemptions. It is pertinent to redirect and redefine economic development strategy with an approach that focuses specifically delimited efforts to promote industries that truly can develop a competitive advantage relative to the rest of the world. The current strategy focuses even promoting Puerto Rico as an advantageous location to the United States, maintaining its comparison on issues that currently appear to be indifferent to companies such as common currency and financial system among others, and ignores the importance of being competitive in the world. It also focuses on promoting a highly skilled workforce, obviating the training capacity and development of knowledge of competitor countries.

A policy of broad economic incentives that is based on the tax exemption with a solid transportation infrastructure with multimodal features and low energy costs are factors that increase competitiveness in the stage of industrial development which classifies Puerto Rico, which is the stage of innovation or industrial development of high technology. Also, a strategy of industrial incentives focused on creating clusters that equates global competition, specifically in relation to Singapore and Malaysia.

It is also necessary to review the granting or not of special incentives to establish industries that administers by Puerto Rico Industrial Development Company. The limited granting of incentives may indicate that the application process and granting it unwieldy for businesses, so they decide not to or benefit from them. It could also indicate that they do not present attractive to motivate companies to go through the application process, evaluation and monitoring of compliance with the agreements which grant. Also the limited granting of incentives may reflect a process of promotion and inadequate evaluation. These factors adversely affect Puerto Rico's incentives policies as a source of competitiveness.

Chapter 5
Outsourcing and Labor in the Manufacturing Sector in Puerto Rico

In today's global business, companies face the challenge of competing both locally and overseas. One option used by some companies to survive against globalization is to outsource non-core portion of its value chain. Outsourcing includes important services for companies, such as information technology, finance and accounting activities. Outsourcing in manufacturing includes intermediates goods (contract manufacturing). Outsourcing represents a form of doing business that transcends the boundaries of a company or a country, and its use affects factors related to manufacturing, including labor. In this chapter the relationship between outsourcing of intermediate goods and labor of the manufacturing sector in Puerto Rico is discussed. Also, is explored the relationship of these factors with capital intensity and return on property, plant and equipment (RPPE) of industries that operate in the Island.

Subcontracting (Outsourcing)

The outsourcing of manufacturing and services to various overseas locations has been increased during the last 20 years (Schniederjans and Zuckweiler 2004). Outsourcing is defined as the acquisition of inputs or activities previously created internally from an external supplier within a long-term contractual relationship, in which only some of the expected mutual benefits and obligations are formally defined (Juma'h and Wood 1999, 2000).

According to Cheng (2007), a greater degree of outsourcing is associated with high financial and operational performance at the industry level. Companies that grant outsourcing contracts are generally engaged in several different activities, in addition to its core business. These companies can reduce their operational expenses by outsourcing non-core activities, as they can focus their resources on the core

---

The chapter is mainly derived from a dissertation conducted by Dr. Landrau-Febres (2013).

A.H. Juma'h et al., *Labor Markets and Multinational Enterprises in Puerto Rico*, SpringerBriefs in Economics, DOI 10.1007/978-3-319-17178-4_5

business in which they have unique economies of skills or knowledge (Jiang et al. 2006, 2007). High wages are positively related to outsourcing, suggesting that the cost saving motive is important (Girma and Görg 2004).

Outsourcing is expected to reduce fixed costs in administrative salaries and cost of inventories (Sen and Zhu 1996). However, it is noted that companies identified as outsourcers have relatively worse operational performance, higher administrative and labor overhead (Paul and Wooster 2010).

Labor intensity may directly influence the value of particular forms of flexible organizations (Schilling and Steensma 2001). It is more likely that labor intensive firms select outsourcing relative to in-sourcing (Tomiura et al. 2011). On the other hand, offshore outsourcing is often considered the root cause of job losses, plant closures, loss of synergetic advantages, loss of innovation capacity, loss of intellectual property, and high dependence on external companies (Mohiuddin et al. 2010).

Labor and Outsourcing

Apparently the use of business practices has a greater impact on labor productivity than on profitability (Percival and Cozzarin 2010). The international division of labor is characterized by companies that are geographically separating different stages of production across the world economy in order to exploit differences in production costs (Marin 2006). However, international restructuring has segmented the production process, fragmented the workforce and transformed firm cost structures in ways that are detrimental to labor (Anner 2011).

It is argued that profitability is the most important criterion to evaluate the performance of a company. Outsourcing, when used properly, can increase profitability in various ways, including staffing, capabilities, facilities and payroll (Jiang et al. 2006).

One disadvantage of outsourcing is the layoff that often result (Chase et al. 1998). Outsourcing can be seen as a substitute for in-house production and may therefore, in the short term, lead to a reduction in the total wage bill (Girma and Görg 2004). Many foreign companies are established where labor costs are low. Its strategic role typically is to manufacture labor intensive products at the lowest possible cost (Hill 2009). When companies outsource, they reduce the range of activities that the domestic industry performs, which can reduce the industry unit demand for less skilled labor (Feenstra and Hanson 1996).

Since the labor costs typically counts as a relatively small percent of the cost of goods sold in many industries, plants with cost reduction strategies may be inclined not to outsource because of the potential complexity of coordinating production with internal logistics and distribution systems (Bardhan et al. 2006). However, it has been assumed that high wage companies do more outsourcing because the cost cutting motive will be more important. But those high wages could respond to higher efficiency due to high skills, resulting in lower unit labor costs. That is, it would be the wage, once productivity differences are taken into account, one of the key drivers of outsourcing (Díaz-Mora 2008). It is estimated that the higher the labor intensity in production and distribution of a product is, the greater the effect of per capita income in the consuming country on product price (Lipsey and Swedenborg 2007). Another factor that may influence the level of markup is the degree of labor intensity, which is defined as the ratio of remuneration of employed to total sales (Rezitis and Kalantzi 2011).

Outsourcing is used to alleviate capacity shortfalls and increase production flexibility (Chang et al. 2008). Moreover, labor intensive can probably lead to higher inventory because of the longer production lead-time (Cheng 2007). The outsourcing intensity is positively related to its labor productivity and total factor productivity growth, and this effect is more pronounced for foreign establishments (Girma and Görg 2004). However, on the other hand it is argued that outsourcing has a negative impact on a company's labor productivity (Broedner et al. 2009).

It is noted that employing individuals or groups of individuals on a short-term contract basis allows an enterprise to readily adjust both its scale and its managerial or technical talent. However, although alternative work arrangements enable companies to quickly bring in new knowledge and skills, they do so at a potential cost (Schilling and Steensma 2001). In addition, using temporary employees may put a firm at greater risk of having its proprietary technologies or competitive tactics spread to other companies. Large companies, measured by the number of employees, with larger organizational costs tend to favor outsourcing; while the most productive companies, relative to the industry average, tend to favor offshoring (Marin 2006).

Outsourcing and Labor in Puerto Rico

According to the data from the Economic Census of Island Areas of the U.S. Census Bureau of the U.S. Department of Commerce and the database of the Office of Economic and Financial Affairs of the Department of the Treasury of Puerto Rico for the years 2002 and 2007, it is possible to gain some insights on outsourcing and labor in Puerto Rico. It is noted that there is a decrease of 12.6 % in the amount of employment generated by manufacturing industries in Puerto Rico. The total payroll of manufacturing reflects a decrease of 4.7 % between 2002 and 2007, which is a signal of the marked reduction in employment. Data on contract labor for production (contract manufacturing) show that there was a decrease in their use of 47.5 % over the period 2002–2007. The major use is for the chemical manufacturing with 36.9 % of the total contract labor for production reported in the Census for 2002, and 37.1 % for 2007; being the pharmaceutical and medicine manufacturing which presents the greatest use. On the other hand, the industrial segment that increased the use of contract labor for production, in percentage terms, was the nonmetallic mineral product manufacturing by 280.3 %; while the sub-sector that diminished their use by 100 % was the textile mills. This suggests that the nonmetallic mineral product manufacturing sub-sector reflects a greater reliance on outsourcing. In 2002 and 2007, the chemical manufacturing presents data with higher values in terms of number of jobs, payroll, contract labor for production and capital expenditures; whose main contribution comes from the pharmaceutical and medicine manufacturing.

Table 5.1 Pearson correlations for CM, RPPE, CI and LI for 2002

Variable		CM	RPPE	CI	LI
CM	r	1			
	S				
	N	21			
RPPE	r	−0.11	1		
	S	0.644			
	N	20	20		
CI	r	−0.157	−0.432*	1	
	S	0.508	0.057		
	N	20	20	20	
LI	r	−0.225	−0.448**	0.403*	1
	S	0.34	0.048	0.078	
	N	20	20	20	20

Note: CM=Contract manufacturing, RPPE=Return on property, plant and equipment, CI=Capital intensity, LI=Labor intensity, r=Pearson correlation coefficient, S=significance (2 tailed), N=Number of observations
*p<0.1, 2 tailed; **p<0.05, 2 tailed; ***p<0.01, 2 tailed

For 2002, the contract manufacturing does not reflect significant correlation with any of the variables included in the analysis. On the other hand, the labor intensity has a significant negative relationship with the RPPE ($r=-0.45$, $p<0.05$); and a positive relationship with the capital intensity ($r=0.40$, $p<0.10$). A negative relationship between capital intensity and RPPE ($r=-0.43$, $p<0.10$) was also observed (see Table 5.1).

For 2007, a significant positive correlation between the contract manufacturing and the capital intensity ($r=0.74$, $p<0.01$) reflected. A significant negative relationship between the contract manufacturing and RPPE is also observed ($r=-0.42$, $p<0.1$). No other relationship was observed between contract manufacturing and the other variables. For that year the labor intensity has a negative relationship with the RPPE ($r=-0.58$, $p<0.01$); and a positive relationship with the capital intensity ($r=0.52$, $p<0.05$). In addition, an inverse relationship between the capital intensity and the RPPE ($r=-0.65$, $p<0.01$) was observed (see Table 5.2).

Conclusions

The companies reported the use of outsourcing of intermediate goods (contract manufacturing) in 2002. However, this type of arrangement between companies was not a determinant strategy to maximize profit in the manufacturing sector in Puerto Rico. Outsourcing may be a tool for meeting commitments, to mitigate capacity insufficiencies and to increase flexibility in production. For 2007, a positive relationship between the contract manufacturing and capital intensity is reflected; and a

Table 5.2 Pearson correlations for CM, RPPE, CI and LI for 2007

Variable		CM	RPPE	CI	LI
CM	r	1			
	S				
	N	21			
RPPE	r	–0.416*	1		
	S	0.076			
	N	19	19		
CI	r	0.736***	–0.649***	1	
	S	0	0.003		
	N	19	19	19	
LI	r	0.334	–0.580***	0.517**	1
	S	0.162	0.009	0.023	
	N	19	19	19	19

Note: CM=Contract manufacturing, RPPE=Return on property, plant and equipment, CI=Capital intensity, LI=Labor intensity, r=Pearson correlation coefficient, S=significance (2 tailed), N=Number of observations

*p<0.1, 2 tailed; **p<0.05, 2 tailed; ***p<0.01, 2 tailed

negative relationship between the contract manufacturing and RPPE is observed; this suggests the use of outsourcing to downsize operations in preparation for a possible relocation of the operations.

For 2002 and 2007, the significant inverse relationship between capital intensity and RPPE suggests a decrease of assets that generates an increase in performance. Meanwhile, the inverse relationship between the labor intensity and RPPE suggests that if the wages are high, it is possible that an increase in the cost of the product may be required to increase the required profit, which in turn would increase the yield on property, plant and equipment. For both years, the capital intensity is positively related to the labor intensity, suggesting the presence of capital intensive companies with high salaries and skilled labor. The availability of skilled labor may indicate that the country has a factor that can provide competitive advantage. The availability of skilled labor encourages the use of this knowledge to benefit by developing strategies, to generate innovation, to adapt quickly to changes and compete in the global manufacturing scenario. This makes it necessary to concentrate on education to continue developing human resources as a factor of competitive advantage.

Chapter 6
Pharmaceutical Industry and R&D in Puerto Rico

In today's advanced technological and competitive era, where globalization takes place, multinational companies expand their competitive advantages to use research and development (R&D). Each market needs to develop new technologies, products, services and processes to face up the economic challenges. The pursuit of competitiveness has led multinational enterprises to develop new strategies to inquire into the key factor for differentiation, using new R&D processes. This chapter discusses R&D and the development of the pharmaceutical industry in Puerto Rico.

R&D and Pharmaceuticals

The pharmaceutical companies are part of the group of multinational companies, which have gained competitive advantages to developing new products and processes to optimize its product portfolio. The R&D process has been one of the mechanisms used to enter in new markets and develop innovative processes. This is also relevant to biotechnology.

The concept of R&D has been used in a large number of investigations as a measure of innovative activity of multinationals. However, there may be discrepancies in the results mainly due to the difficulty in measuring innovation activity. One of the most popular ways to measure innovation is using companies' spending on R&D. Spending on R&D in the pharmaceutical belonging to the Pharmaceutical Research and Manufacturers of America (PHRMA) accounted for about $48.5 billion in 2012 (PIE 2013). This indicates to the importance and growth of R&D activities in the pharmaceutical industry (see Table 6.1).

The chapter is derived from a dissertation done by Dr. Torres-Morales (2013) and other presentations and works realized by INDUNIV Consortium (2013) and PIE (2013).

A.H. Juma'h et al., *Labor Markets and Multinational Enterprises in Puerto Rico*, SpringerBriefs in Economics, DOI 10.1007/978-3-319-17178-4_6

Table 6.1 R&D spending by PHRMA members

Year	US$ billions
2012	48.5
2011	48.6
2010	50.7
2009	46.4
2008	47.4
2007	47.9
2006	43.4
2005	39.9
2000	26.0
1990	8.4
1980	2.0

Source: Adapted from the presentation of the Pharmaceutical Industry Executives at the Annual Meeting of the Puerto Rico Economist Association, August 30, 2013

R&D represents a very heavy economic burden for companies seeking to innovate. To stay competitive in the industry, pharmaceuticals need to keep their growing product portfolio, so that when patents expire main drugs can substitute with other drugs approved. As such the pharmaceutical industry is highly regulated and with extensive and expensive R&D process, pharmaceuticals constantly need to innovate. The innovation process is carried out in different countries and varies according to the companies. The R&D centers in the pharmaceutical industry are mostly in the United States, but many have a presence in European and Asian countries. This movement has been both establishing R&D centers and manufacturing relocation to countries where they have these research centers (see Table 6.2).

Because of its great intensity in R&D, the pharmaceutical industry has been one of the research topics of economists. This has been examined from different research approaches, including pricing strategy, the intensity of competition, economies of scale, economies of scope, and innovation activity. In recent years it has been part of the new economy in the global arena. Not only have developed new drugs, used in many cases large budgets for R&D, otherwise pharmaceuticals have established research and manufacturing in various parts of the world, such as India, China, Singapore and Ireland, among other countries that perceived as fully developed for these purposes. However, the economic development of these countries has led to major pharmaceutical companies to establish and develop new facilities with large investments, giving a boost to the local economy of each country, especially with the establishment of new centers of biotechnology.

However, many countries have been adversely affected by these new R&D centers, due to the closure of operations within their borders and re-establishments in other locations. Among these countries is Puerto Rico. In recent years, several pharmaceutical operations have ceased. For example GlaxoSmithKline and Wyeth no longer have a presence on the Island, and in 2009, Pfizer acquired Wyeth in a

Table 6.2 Countries with R&D center of companies with some operations in Puerto Rico

Pharmaceuticals	Countries with R&D centers
Pfizer	USA, UK
GlaxoSmithKline	US, France, Spain, Italy, Croatia, China, UK
Sanofi-Aventis	US, Canada, France, Germany, Hungry, Japan, UK, Italy, Spain
Novartis	USA, Switzerland, Italia, China, Japan, Indonesia, Singapore, India, UK
AstraZeneca	USA, Canada, France, Sweden, Japan, India, UK
Johnson & Johnson	USA, Spain, France, Belgium Switzerland, China, India, UK
Merck	USA, Canada, Italia, France, Japan, UK
Roche	USA, Canada, Austria, Germany, Switzerland, Japan, China, UK, Australia
Eli Lilly	USA, Canada, Spain, Japan, China, UK, Australia, Singapore
Wyeth[a]	USA, Ireland, Japan, China, Africa, Australia
Abbott	USA, Germany, Japan, China, Singapore
Bristol-Myers Squibb	USA, France, Belgium, UK
Schering-Plough[b]	USA, Scotland, Germany, France, Japan

[a]In 2009 merged with Pfizer
[b]In 2009 merged with Merck

transaction of $68 billion, and has recently closed some of its plants. Other pharmaceutical as Abbott, Amcor, Boston Scientific, Ivax Pharmaceuticals, Ortho Pharmaceuticals and Patheon announced relocations during the period from 2005 to 2012. Other personnel have decreased considerably. These changes have had different effects on the industry and the economy of Puerto Rico.

In many cases, pharmaceutical companies have withdrawn from Puerto Rico for lack of successful competitive strategies, loss of patents, the fierce competition of bio-equivalent, lack of approval from the US Food and Drug Administration (FDA) of new products and the high costs of R&D. Furthermore, loss of the benefits of Section 936 the emergence of global, such as more regulatory controls less success rate in bringing treatments to market and increases in production costs will be added pressures. Each of these problems has worsened over the years, and has pushed the pharmaceutical industry to find new strategies for the development and maintenance of their products (Custodio 2010).

Employment and Economic Activity in the Pharmaceutical Industry of Puerto Rico

The pharmaceutical industry in Puerto Rico has been one of the fastest growing industries in the past four decades. Traditionally, this industry is one that has contributed most to exports and employment to manufacturing industry in Puerto Rico. For the period 2006–2012, the industry contributed between 20 and 25 % of jobs in the manufacturing sector.[1] In 2006 the pharmaceutical industry even claimed around 30,000 direct jobs in Puerto Rico, representing 26 % of total manufacturing jobs. It also represented 26.5 % of GDP in Puerto Rico and generated 60 % of total exports of the Island.

In Puerto Rico, 20 world leading pharmaceuticals are established and manufacture 16 of the top 20 drugs of the US market. The pharmaceutical industry in Puerto Rico has concentrated on the manufacture of pharmaceuticals, biotechnology and medical devices. The pharmaceutical industry has maintained four competitive industries on the Island including medicinal and botanical products; pharmaceutical preparations; surgical and medical instruments; and electronic components for medical use.

Pharmaceutical companies operating in Puerto Rico have centers of R&D for new products outside the Island. Subsidiaries located on the Island are mostly extensions of manufacturing operations, where a variety of products distributed locally in the US and foreign markets. Furthermore, activities in the pharmaceutical sector generates about 68,000 indirect jobs and promote jobs in the rest of the economy, such as professional organizations, various services including jobs are in banking, engineering, insurance, transportation and communication (PIA 2011).

However, the industry has shown an important reduction in job creation. The decrease in the number of jobs in the manufacture of pharmaceutical products in recent years has been evident; by 2005 the number of jobs in the pharmaceutical industry stood at 28,200 jobs and by 2012 had 16,700 jobs, which represents a decrease of about 11,500 jobs over a period of 7 years (Planning Board 2012).

Despite the reduction of jobs in industry, pharmaceutical exports continue to represent a large portion of total exports of Puerto Rico. In 2012, exports of pharmaceutical products accounted for 69 % of total exports (see Fig. 6.1) and 28 % of GDP. Also, to contributed about 34 % of jobs in the manufacturing sector. A greatest in economic sectors multiplier effect on job creation of 3.3 is estimated. Similarly, it is estimated that 79 % of revenues of the Treasury of Puerto Rico comes from taxes paid by the industry (INDUNIV 2013).

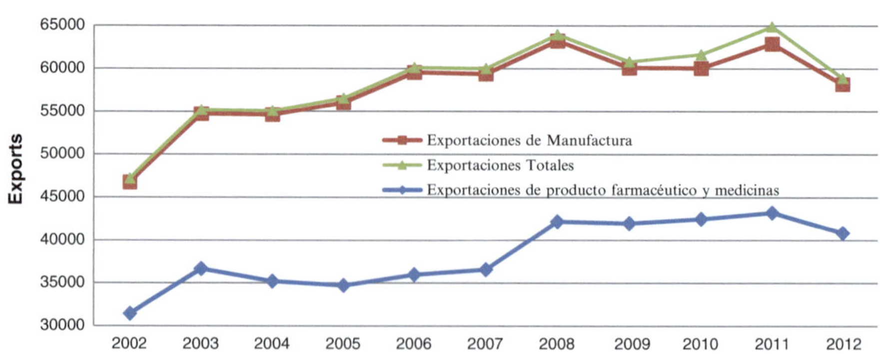

Fig. 6.1 Puerto Rico exports during 2002–2012

[1] Planning Board of Puerto Rico (2012).

R&D and the Pharmaceutical Industry in Puerto Rico

It is noted that the efforts of the Government of Puerto Rico to strengthen value-added activities in the biotechnology sector is one devoid of guarantees for the pharmaceutical long term activity on the Island due to an erosion of the global market. It argues that the Island faces the threat of development and manufacturing of medicines in low-cost jurisdictions such as India and China. It also faces the loss of competitiveness in the R&D sector in countries like Ireland and Singapore. Furthermore, changes in tax incentives at the local level have also weakened the mood of industry for economic activity in Puerto Rico. Considering adverse aspects, the financial crisis of local government is also added. This situation is added to other events such as the maturity of the exemptions provided by Section 936 in 2006 and the increasing of labor costs (Business Monitor International 2006; Morales et al. 2012).

As presented by the Pharmaceutical Industry Executives some of the considerations for establishing both pharmaceutical operations and R&D include the following factors: the transaction costs, the economy, infrastructure, human resource, quality of life, technology, enabling environment for trade, education, cost of living and access to capital (PIE 2013). When analyzing the economic indicators of the countries with high establishment of the pharmaceutical R&D, these countries offer incentives and have a number of economic advantages over Puerto Rico; they have competitive advantages to multinationals for R&D center establishment. The economic indicators show how these countries are developing positively, with low unemployment rates and positive growth of GDP. Similarly, educational indicators can be used as a measure or important for the establishment of R&D centers factor. Higher education plays a key role in innovation, important part of R&D. Also, the location of the best universities in the world matches the host countries of R&D centers.

Puerto Rico despite having a pharmaceutical presence of many years in as manufacturing operations has not been fully developed in R&D. In Puerto Rico, basic research that do not generate patents are held. However, currently only has a limited amount of R&D centers, 12 in total (see Fig. 6.2). Of these, seven centers were established as a result of R&D incentives granted by Law 73 of 2008 (i.e. Law on Economic Incentives for Economic Development of Puerto Rico).

Also, some universities have limited investment in R&D funds. In addition, several companies are developing biotechnology activities on the Island (see Table 6.3). However, the lack of data on economic indicators and the R&D activities on the Puerto Rico do not help to promote the importance of R&D in the economy.

To compete in the new global economy and to compete with countries like Singapore, Malaysia, Ireland, Finland, India and Indonesia, it is recommended to direct efforts to promote and develop a knowledge-based economy. Puerto Rico has begun to develop initiatives in the development of knowledge. As part of the efforts that have been developed are partnerships with universities, academic programs in biotechnology and the collection of data on R&D in Puerto Rico by the Statistical Office of Puerto Rico.

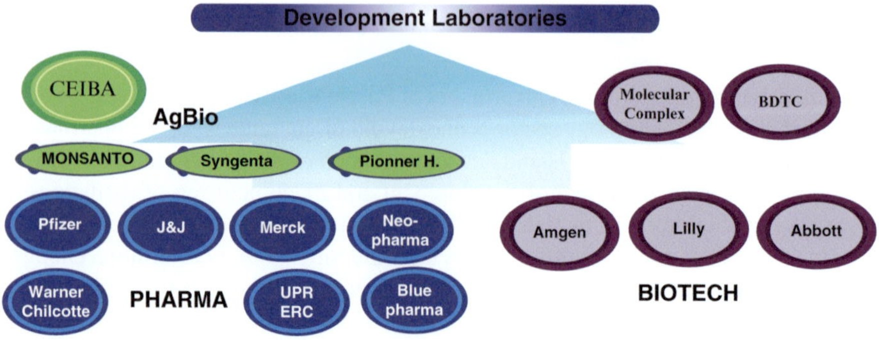

Fig. 6.2 R&D centers in Puerto Rico. *Source*: Adapted from the presentation The Life Science Industry, INDUNIV Research Consortium, 2013

Table 6.3 Bio-pharmaceuticals operation in Puerto Rico

Abbott Pharma operations/Barceloneta	J&J/McNeil Healthcare LLC: Las Piedras
AbbVie/Barceloneta	J&J/Ortho Biologics—Manatí
AbbVie/Jayuya	J&J/Ortho Pharmaceuticals—Manatí
Amgen/Juncos	Merck Sharp & Dohme/Arecibo
AstraZeneca/Canóvanas	Merck Sharp & Dohme/Barceloneta
Bristol Myers Squibb/Humacao	Merck Sharp & Dohme/Las Piedras
Bristol Myers Squibb/Manatí	Novartis Ex-Lax/Humacao
Eli Lilly del Caribe/Carolina	Pfizer/Barceloneta
Eli Lilly del Caribe/Guayama	Pfizer/Vega Baja
Eli Lilly del Caribe Biotechnology/Carolina	Pfizer Consumer (Wyeth)/Guayama
J&J/Ethicon LLC—San Lorenzo	Warner Chilcott/Fajardo
J&J/Janssen Ortho LLC—Gurabo	Warner Chilcott/Manatí
J&J/Lifescan Products—Aguadilla	

Source: Adapted from the presentation of the Pharmaceutical Industry Executives at the Annual Meeting of the Puerto Rico Economist Association, August 30, 2013

The partnership between the University of Puerto Rico and the MD Anderson Cancer Center (located in Texas and known for its comprehensive center dedicated exclusively to the treatment, research, education and prevention of cancer), for purposes of research and treatment of the Hispanic population is such example. Puerto Rico participation in R&D is limited and disadvantage over other competitors, yet efforts increase. It is starting to generate an infrastructure aimed at the knowledge economy and is expected to innovation activity in the Island increase in the years to come (see Fig. 6.3).

The pharmaceutical industry in Puerto Rico is an important and integral part of the economy and if a significant reduction of it is occurred, the results would be unfavorable for the whole economy of Puerto Rico. Among the negative effects are the unemployment rate would rise and GDP is significantly reduced.

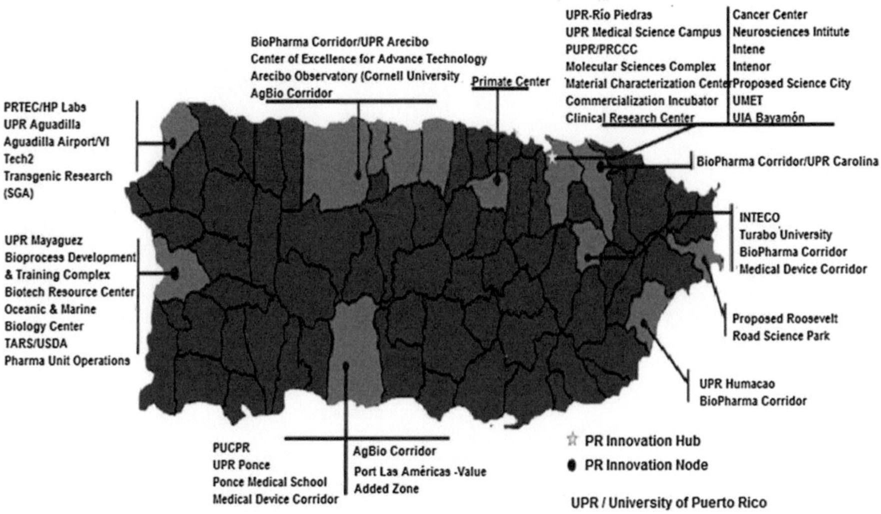

Fig. 6.3 Puerto Rico innovation center map. *Source*: Adapted from the presentation The Life Science Industry, INDUNIV Research Consortium, 2013

The competitiveness of Puerto Rico is declining. Possible factors for the loss of competitiveness include the political uncertainty in Puerto Rico, high energy costs and lack of partners in scientific research. These factors lead to a difficult Puerto Rico when attracting new projects for the manufacture of products (Guillen 2009) situation.

The Island still has the presence in pharmaceutical manufacturing of the best in the world and produces a large amount of drugs with overall higher market sales. Moreover, in recent years have prompted efforts to maintain the presence of existing companies and develop new areas such as biotechnology and R&D. But Puerto Rico is not the only country to develop these efforts. Countries like Taiwan, Malaysia and Singapore have aimed their efforts to develop biotechnology. Aspects such as a strategic location to develop pharmaceutical and biotechnology industries contribute to the positioning of competing countries like Ireland and Singapore. Also, the economic incentives that these two countries offer may be similar to those of Puerto Rico.

Despite the disrupted of Section 936, Puerto Rico still has a skilled workforce, a work tradition focused on quality, infrastructure facilities and high-level communication. Industry executives indicated that they still observe a level of competitiveness that can be aimed to the development of specific sectors in the industry, so the refocus of the pharmaceutical industry in Puerto Rico is proposed, one directed to the manufacture of generic drugs.

The generics market represents an area of growth and opportunity for Puerto Rico. Generic drugs accounted for 80 % of the global market for 2012, and it is projected to continue to grow (see Fig. 6.4). It is noted that the Island still has some strengths that contribute significantly to competitiveness and make it attractive to

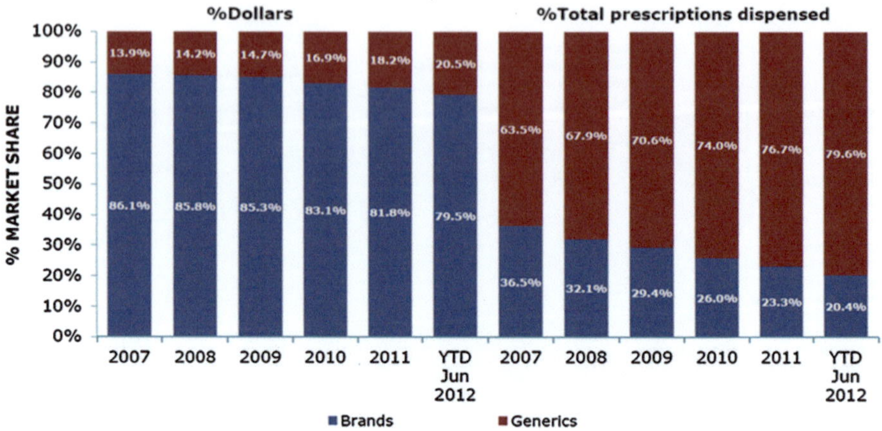

Fig. 6.4 Market growth of generics. *Source*: IMS Health, National Sales Perspectives, June 2012, National Prescription Audit, June 2012, disaggregated Branded generics. Presented by the PIE at the Annual Meeting of the Puerto Rico Economists Association on August 30, 2013

develop a generic industry (PIE 2013). These strengths are listed as: high technical knowledge, acuity and managerial experience, plants (infrastructure) available, diversity of human resources, lots of universities and technical colleges, some centers of R&D existing infrastructure for water, electricity and communications, location and logistics system, and the new Investment Act (PIE 2013). Furthermore, a high expertise arises in the process of quality control that leads to Puerto Rico in compliance with FDA regulations over other competing countries, especially India and China face.

On other hand, some weakness are identified that include poor education of English language and mathematics, poor entrepreneurship, deficiencies in the use of tools and improvement processes, the lack of a development of long term plan and agility to issued licenses and permits (PIE 2013). But business groups in the pharmaceutical industry; betting convert Puerto Rico in generic drugs manufacturing center.

Conclusions

Puerto Rico faces the decline of the manufacturing sector and its main industry branch, the pharmaceutical industry. The loss of competitiveness and macroeconomic factors contribute to this situation. This raises the need for assertive strategies to address the negative implications for the economy, such as reducing jobs and GDP.

It is necessary not only to establish strategies for the retention of established pharmaceutical plants, but also completely re-focus the development strategy and industrial promotion. Apparently the address could be more feasible in this new strategy is based on developing a generic manufacturing, in which the business community itself has identified some competitive advantages for Puerto Rico compared to those competitors and emerging countries, particularly Ireland, Singapore and Malaysia.

It is also important to increase the activity of R&D on the Island. Although formulated initiatives in order to promote the establishment of centers of R&D and the creation of new knowledge, they may not be enough, so it is necessary to evaluate and redirect these measures.

Chapter 7
A Global Perspective

It is notable that the population of Puerto Rico had decreased in the last 10 years. For example, during the 1980s the population was 3.9 million and for 2012 estimated at 3.5 million. The decrease in population reflects important aspects about the deteriorating economy. Many Puerto Ricans migrate mainly to the United States in search of economic and employment opportunities. Data on gross national product per capita shows a nominal increase of $11,823.3 in 2001 to $18.872 in 2012. However, if we take the per capita gross national product at constant prices of 1954 reflected that in 2001 is $1,801.6 and 2012 was $1,750 showing a decrease.

The labor participation rate in Puerto Rico is less than other competing countries of in the manufacturing sector. According to World Bank data, Puerto Rico is located as the seventh country with the lowest labor participation rate in the world. The main competitors (Malaysia, Mexico, Dominican Republic, Singapore and Ireland) have participation rates above 60 %, while that of Puerto Rico is 40 %. This limited participation in the labor market and the low productivity of labor in Puerto Rico, is partly due to the conditioning of the population, led to dependence on social assistance subsidized by federal transfers.

Puerto Rico has had changes in the inflow of FDI, for example in 1980 was $657 million and for 2010 was $5,043 million. Comparing the proportional growth in relation to Ireland (FDI in 1980 was $286 million and for 2010 was $26,330 million see Table 3.1), it is noticeable that this other country is better positioned to attract FDI. In addition, an increase in the Gross Domestic Product (GDP) and exports pass by almost double those of Puerto Rico is evident. There is a positive relationship between FDI and employment rate, which shows the importance of FDI for job creation and economic growth of countries.

The global positioning of the Island is related to loss of competitiveness in attracting foreign direct investment. This is reflected in shipments of operations of multinational companies. In recent years many companies have made relocation to various countries, including on economic incentives offered and awarded by the Government of Puerto Rico. An economic development strategy based solely on offering economic incentives seems not sufficient to attract and retain multinational

A.H. Juma'h et al., *Labor Markets and Multinational Enterprises in Puerto Rico*, SpringerBriefs in Economics, DOI 10.1007/978-3-319-17178-4_7

companies. Therefore, it is possible to argue that the economic incentives of the Island are not attractive enough when compared to the added value of a strong transportation infrastructure, low energy costs, a less expensive labor and the opportunity to access wide local and international market among other factors such as economic incentives offered by competing countries.

It is evident that multinationals have used the highly trained workforce in Puerto Rico in recent decades as part of the value chain in pharmaceutical production, but establishing R&D centers on the Island still limited. So, polices of the Government of Puerto Rico aimed at increasing the activities and the establishment of R&D operations has not been effective in achieve their stated goal. They seem to be insufficient for multinationals to establish these activities on the Island. Despite this, Puerto Rico was the eighth scientific content of documents cited in Latin America for 2013. Scientific research has been presented in areas of medicine, physics and astronomy, biological sciences, agriculture, biochemistry, genetics, molecular biology and materials science (Christante de Mello 2014).

Organizations like INDUNIV say the Science and Technology Trust created by 214 Act of August 18, 2004, does not have the necessary funds to make a significant contribution to boost and position the Island as a world center for the development of activities. INDUNIV argues that to compete in attracting local R&D, it is estimated that Puerto Rico needs to have at least $1 billion in funds and joint support system with effective networks to develop capital, develop business initiatives and protect intellectual property.

Recently, economic activities of multinationals in Puerto Rico have been affected by changes in global market such as reduction in borders to cross and distances between countries Technological advances have helped companies diversify their operations and further internationalize their production in order to maintain their competitive advantage.

Although the Island has a highly skilled workforce and global quality management capacity, there is an even higher level of competition for this type of labor, especially in countries with technology-intensive industries and extensive activities in R&D. According to new theories of development, multinationals use resources in different countries to minimize operating costs and maximize economies of scale. One of the practices by these companies is the outsourcing of manufacturing and services. It has been noted that the contracted intermediate manufacturing goods in 2007 had a positive relationship with the intensity of capital. Also, there is a negative relationship between the contracted intermediate manufacturing goods and performance on property, plant and equipment, which may indicate that outsourcing is used as a management strategy to reduce the size of operations in preparation for possible relocations or closure of operations.

In addition, there has been an inverse relationship between the intensity of labor and return on property, plant and equipment which may show relatively high spending on labor (as a positive relationship between capital intensity and labor intensity). This supports a high cost in labor tends to increase the cost of product so that companies can experience reductions in their income (profit). This may represent the loss of global competitiveness of companies. One consequence of this is that companies can make strategic decisions that will maintain them competitive cost levels so they achieve an advantageously in the international market. An alternative to regain global competitiveness is to outsource the manufacturing or services.

The economic development strategy that positioned Puerto Rico and ushered in industrialization shepherded many of the countries that currently lead the manufacturing industry. Attracting FDI by granting economic incentives and cheap labor was emulated by countries like Singapore, Malaysia and Ireland. However, if we compare the economic development policies of these countries and Puerto Rico, these countries developed strategies to specific industries, particularly to attract high-technology industries and R&D. Moreover, these countries selected sectors should sustain its structural transformation and focused their fiscal resources to develop an entrepreneurial culture and an appropriate labor market.

In addition to establishing significant economic incentives and robust backup system for the value chain, these countries have used education as an essential axis of its economic development strategy. Mostly these countries reflect an integrated industry and focused on the development of science education, mathematics, languages and professions in line with its economic development strategy. Also, their institutional structures are organized to make possible the process of development and the establishment of industries.

Unlike other countries, Puerto Rico has not yet formulated a strategy for economic development that meets the new global landscape. The strategy set by the "Bootstrap" project proved successful until the late 1970s, but it responded to a completely different world order. The foundations of Operation Bootstrap were not used in time to make the transition to the next stage of industrialization. Although this model was effective in boosting economic growth and for the Island and creating a competence base, there is no formulated strategy for long term economic growth appropriate for developing industries based on knowledge and technology.

Many factors have contributed to the strategic dislocation model of Puerto Rico. We can point to two main causes that have proved pivotal in this matter; the political status of the Island with the United States and strategic conditioning to government changes in electoral processes. Countries that have achieved success in their economic development strategies and can be comparable to Puerto Rico, for its size and population (meaning Singapore and Ireland) are countries with a political definition that allows them to establish a business and an economic policy without entering in contradiction that could alter its order. Similarly, these countries have set their strategies with a futuristic and long-term vision. Making adjustments in the short and medium term in response to temporary needs but, according to the established model, not subject to the current political moment.

Puerto Rico faces great challenges, but the greatest of all is to quickly articulate a development strategy to mobilize the economy. It is recommended to concentrate its resources and efforts to be competitive in areas that actually still have areas of opportunity. In previous chapters, we have identified some elements that could be part of that strategy. Manufacturing remains a vital part of the economy of Puerto Rico. Need to identify those manufacturing activities in which the Island has comparative advantage. It is also advisable to identify service activities that can be outsourced to other countries. Also, increasing efforts to promote a knowledge economy in Puerto Rico so that R&D can be established.

Particularly, the pharmaceutical industry is considered one of the major players in the development of Puerto Rico. We have identified an area of opportunity for the establishment of generic manufacturing it is important to consider. There are local industry efforts to promote the development of generic drugs, supporting the potential for success based on the expertise in quality control and federal regulations developed through experience, availability of plants that are adapted to the specifications industry and the common market and integration with the United States. The potential growth of the industry is also argued, but in turn, the magnitude of the initial investment for the establishment of plants is between $50 and $60 million per plant and has an estimated return on investment of between 3 and 5 years. So the biggest challenge for the establishment and development of this industry is the availability of local capital and attracting foreign capital.

It is important that Puerto Rico concentrate its resources and efforts in a concerted and systematic long-term plan. Over the last years economic policies have been diluted in the various sectors of the economy, not responding to an objective of leadership in any of them. Nearby countries like Dominican Republic, Panama and Colombia have managed to respond better to changes, beating Puerto Rico in their economic growth trends.

To achieve a better global positioning must be addressed various aspects. The level of education is crucial to retain businesses and increase the level of production on the Island. Globally ties between universities and multinational companies are increasing, particularly in the areas of research. Research centers supported by industries are examples of partnerships between industry and universities. This helps to develop curricula more suited to the needs of labor. However, in Puerto Rico this integration just takes his first steps. Although some organizations are making efforts to integrate industry, academia and government, it still seems that it is not sufficient for a targeted, systematic and effective strategy. It is necessary to strengthen these efforts, but even more, universities should be open to refocus and renew their offerings and academic activities in sync with the needs of industry.

It is imperative that the government restructure the education system as a whole and adopt advanced educational models to increase human capital. The redesigning the education system in all its components is recommended: educational focus, organizational structure, profile of human resources (teachers) and revalue it in relation to its strategic role in economic and social development of Puerto Rico.

The cost of labor in manufacturing production in Puerto Rico is much more expensive in proportion to that of its main competitors (Mexico, Dominican Republic, Singapore and Malaysia). In addition to this high nominal cost, is also considered as labor regulations that further increase the cost of this factor. The adoption of a federal minimum wage contributed to the loss of competitiveness of the Island, becoming less profitable operations intensive manufacturing workforce. Countries like Singapore and Ireland have established policies that promote a flexible labor market where labor-management relationship is governed on the basis of productivity and the needs of the industry the employer is able to hire, fire, and reward staff based on productivity parameters.

Studies such as the Federal Reserve Bank of New York in 2012, raised the possibility of establishing in Puerto Rico a system based on a sub-minimum wage to promote recruitment of low-skill manpower and/or youth in Puerto Rico. It is also recommended to promote a system to the labor force to reduce the levels welfare dependence can be reduced. Also, skills development should be facilitated and the amount of aid granted should be related to the productive capacity of the person.

It is important that labor legislation in Puerto Rico is concerted and integrated to public policy for economic development. There has been a tendency to formulate public policy for the labor sector that is contradictory to the needs of improving competitiveness. The efficiency of the labor market is a central part of economic activity on the Island. It is also recommend a review of labor law to make adjustments such that a more friendly economic environment for foreign investors and local industry can be achieved.

The energy cost has become one of the major factors for competitiveness in the recent decade. Because the energy in Puerto Rico is generated mostly by use of petroleum, the rise in the price of that in recent years has adversely affected the cost of energy. In addition, the system supplied power is provided by a single firm, the Puerto Rico Electric Power Authority (PREPA).

According to the Electric Power Authority, in 2005 the average cost for industrial energy in Puerto Rico was 14.6 cents per kwh, an average of 1,648 industrial customers and an average consumption of 354.8 mkwh amount remained, while already in by 2012 the average cost of industrial energy was 26.3 cents per kwh, the amount of industrial customers dropped to an average of 721.25 clients as well as the average consumption also fell to 208.36 mkwh. This reduction shows the decline in industrial activity on the Island, partly a result of the relocation of multinational operations to other locations.

For the past 20 years the Government of Puerto Rico has discussed the issue of energy considering various alternatives that make more efficient this sector. The generation using petroleum has become one of the topics of greatest interest, since these increases the cost of living and production costs. However, this problem has not been solved and power generation system continues using petroleum and a single provider. Currently, the overall restructuring of this system is one of the main issue that capturing the attention of all Puerto Ricans. There is need of energy to reduce cost are considered such as natural gas. Other clean and renewable alternative source to generate energy to reduce cost are considered such as solar, wind and ethanol.

This situation becomes even more relevant to changes in federal environmental regulations known as the Clean Air Act, which requires the EPA[1] to set National Ambient Air Quality Standards. This requires that Puerto Rico into compliance with the new standards in April 2015, implying an estimated cost of $1.5 billion for the acquisition of equipment for emissions control, plus an increase in the cost of operation and maintenance. This implies that the system continue in the current direction would be an increase in production costs even higher for the industrial

[1] US Environmental Protection Agency.

sector, and the need for capital investment to comply with EPA regulations (CICAAE 2012). This is a further issue that reduces the competitiveness of Puerto Rico for attracting and retaining FDI and the capacity of local industry to compete and maintain their economic activity.

Various options are being analyzed by the authorities. The opening of the energy market potential on the Island is raised, although opponents of the proposal say the market size is very limited and it will not be successful. Competitors like Singapore and Malaysia have an energy system provided by various suppliers, by generating renewable energy and reduced use of fossil fuels and oil derivatives. The role of government is a regulator of these companies. Puerto Rico should face this situation as an urgent issue and take measures to seriously increase its competitiveness. Otherwise the industrial sector is going to continue shrink with devastating implications for the economy.

Through various studies included in this work could be identified weaknesses in government organizational structure responsible for the implementation and evaluation public policy for the economic development of Puerto Rico. Lack of integration (information and processes) between PRIDCO, Industrial Tax Exemption Office, Treasury Department, Department of Labor and Human Resources and Puerto Rico Trade and Export Company among others. These units responsible for promoting and implementing economic and labor policies on the Island do not work in a coordinated manner. They do not share a database nor have a uniform data collection system. There is a gap in the database of these Agencies since they are not interconnected. An example of this is that the information about on plants collected by the Unit for Displaced Workers and Employers to the Labor Development Administration, Department of Labor and Human Resources, which is collected by legal mandate at least of 60 days before any closing or reorganizations of plants is not reported or shared with the PRIDCO and the Industrial Tax Exemption Office. This information is useful for the design of retention strategies directed at these companies. Also, it has utility for managing buildings PRIDCO lease companies. In many cases companies leave the Island and do not report their departure, so a proper process of rescission of the lease and/or delivery of the building doesn't take place.

It is important to create government cohesion. It is advisable to integrate the databases of all the agencies that have responsibility in implementing economic policy of Puerto Rico. It is recommended that the organic law of the Treasury Department which sets strict controls for the dissemination of taxpayer information is reviewed. These controls usually represent impediments for data analysis by other dependencies on the performance and compliance of companies. In addition, information is empirical evidence or indicative assertive in formulating public policies.

It is advisable to evaluate the entire structure that promotes the development policy of the Government of Puerto Rico and adjust it to the new strategy to be adopted as a project and vision for global positioning of the Island. It is required an evaluation and restructuring of the entire promotion process of Puerto Rico as a destination for business and establishing operations. Also the whole process of granting and monitoring compliance with economic incentives needs to be evaluated so that better suit the purposes for which they are designed.

The efficient process to establish business enterprises is a key element that affects the competitiveness of Puerto Rico to the world. Excessive government bureaucracy has been identified as the main barrier to the competitiveness of the Island to do business by the World Economic Forum (2013). In recent years there have been several revisions to the processes and the permits required to do business in Puerto Rico, however, still remains as a delaying factor that is costly and time-consuming to employers and entrepreneurs. The ineffectiveness of the process is due in part to the lack of government cohesion and lack of strategic direction of Puerto Rico. It is vital for the proper performance of the economy of Puerto Rico that processes are restructured in line with successful economic development strategy. It is recommended that this process is minimizes this process so that invite and promote the proliferation of multinational and local companies in identified strategic sectors.

It is important to raise awareness in Puerto Rico about the need make life changes. This includes individual participation as productive being the economic development of the Island, through appropriate and focused academic preparation in areas where the individual can contribute to the competitive advantage of Puerto Rico. Of course, it is recommended that the Government of Puerto Rico initiate an educational propaganda strategy that citizens understand the importance of their contribution to solving the economic problems of the Island and boost the economy.

The competitiveness of Puerto Rico should pursue not just a re-focus on the production structure, institutional reorganization, modernization and enhancement of infrastructure, reducing costs of production factors, but also a true social and individual change. This is achieved through formal education, democratic values and rule of law.

Advisory Board of the Puerto Rico Manufacturers Association Comments

This work is supported by the Puerto Rico Manufactures Association via its Advisory Board comprise of leading industry leaders, which included the following comments.

Héctor Jiménez-Juarbe, Esq.[1]

Comment:

"This document helps understand the importance of the multinational corporations in Puerto Rico, and invites to explore the possibility of them becoming a catapult for an integrated, industrial economic growth that promotes the continuous development of a strong, local manufacturing and service sectors".

Bartolmé Gamundi, Engr.[2]

Comment:

"An indispensable an unique book that beside covering the development and contribution of multinational companies in Puerto Rico, also is a tool for the definition of strategies and policies to further develop our competiveness capabilities of attracting foreign investment and incorporating the local manufacturing and service corporation in to a fully integrated value chain."

---

[1] Héctor Jiménez Juarbe was CEO of the Puerto Rico Manufacturers Association for 29 years. He is the former Executive Director of PRIDCO. He also served in other important executive posts at the Transportation and Public Works Department and the Highway Authority of Puerto Rico.

[2] Bartolomé Gamundi was Secretary of the Puerto Rico Department of Economic Development and Commerce and President of Commerce and Export Company of Puerto Rico. He is the former General Manager at Electro Biology Corp., Arthur Andersen, Price Waterhouse, GE and Weston Instrument. Gamundi is a former President of Puerto Rico Manufacturers Association and Puerto Rico Chamber of Commerce. He was member of the committee that drafted 73 Act of May 28, 2008.

A.H. Juma'h et al., *Labor Markets and Multinational Enterprises in Puerto Rico*, SpringerBriefs in Economics, DOI 10.1007/978-3-319-17178-4

William Riefkohl, Esq.[3]

Comments on Chapter 4:

"Read this interesting chapter brought to my mind the following observation: At the end of the Second World War, Puerto Rico began its industrialization program, which was to make use of the non-applicability to Puerto Rico of the federal tax system, in order to provide exemption from local taxes and other assistance to foreign companies that established factories on the Island to manufacture any new product or a series of designated products already produced here. The program, called Operation Bootstrap ("Operación Manos a la Obra") was very successful and Puerto Rico soon began to grow at levels previously unimagined. This program was studied and emulated by several foreign countries, including Ireland and Singapore. Puerto Rico held the lead for a long time, but then Ireland and Singapore caught up and exceeded in all indicators, a phenomenon that continues to this day. By analyzing and studying this process, a fact highlighted: Ireland's economy has developed linked to all the countries of Europe and to the United States, Singapore's economy is linked to all the countries of Asia and to the United States that of Puerto Rico is only linked to the United States."

Comments on Chapter 6:

"This chapter is very incisive. It is present a new perspective to an issue that has been part of my entire professional life. Puerto Rico's effort to develop an economy based on R & D, which we have called knowledge economy, may have failed to having repeatedly knocked at the wrong doors. While the main focus of attention remains in those economic sectors whose decisional centers are not in Puerto Rico, the results will be slow, uneven and few. Without abandoning this goal, it is time for Puerto Rico capitalizes on those sectors where it has a native base with experience and power and local decisional capacity to enter the world of R & D on a firm and true mode. To do this, it must center with the engineering and food sectors".

[3] William Riefkohl was Executive Vice President and CEO to the Puerto Rico Manufacturers Association. He is former Executive Director of PRIDCO. He facilitated the creation of the Institute of Science and Technology.

References

214 Act—Ley para Crear el Fideicomiso de Ciencia, Tecnología e Investigación de Puerto Rico, Ley 214 de 18 de agosto de 2004, según enmendada. http://wwwlexjuris.com/lextex/leyes2004/lexl200414.htm

73 Act—Ley de Incentivos Económicos de Puerto Rico, Ley 73 de 28 de mayo de2008, según enmendada. http://www.presupuesto.gobierno.pr/PresupuestosAnteriores/af2009_2010/Tom_II/suppdocs/baselegal/195/073-2008.pdf

Akaike H (1974) A new look at the statistical model identification. IEEE Trans Autom Contr 19(6):716–723

Akaike H (1981) Likelihood of a model and information criteria. J Econom 16:3–14

Aktar I, Ozturk L (2009) Can unemployment be cured by economic growth and foreign direct investment in Turkey? Int Res J Fin Econ 27:203–211

Alameda J (2000) El mercado laboral en Puerto Rico: fundamentos básicos, análisis e interpretación. Ceterisparibus 2. http://ceteriparibus.uprm.edu/articulos/vol2/mercado-laboral.htm

Alameda Lozada J, González Martínez A (2001) Cambio Tecnológico, Productividad y Crecimiento Económico en Puerto Rico. Unidad de Investigaciones Económicas de la Universidad de Puerto Rico, Universidad de Puerto Rico, Río Piedras

Anner M (2011) The impact of international outsourcing on unionization and wages: evidence from the apparel export sector in Central America. Ind Lab Rel Rev 64(2):305–322

Aponte E (1999) Hacia una política y desarrollo de una infraestructura de información y conocimiento para la implantación de la estrategia económica de Puerto Rico. In: Martínez FE (ed) Futuro Económico de Puerto Rico: Antología de ensayos del Proyecto Universitario Sobre el Futuro Económico de Puerto Rico. Editorial de la Universidad de Puerto Rico, San Juan

Aponte E (2005) La Economía de Puerto Rico en la Economía Global y la Educación Superior. Cuaderno de Investigación en la Educación, 20 (diciembre). Centros de Investigaciones Educativas, Universidad de Puerto Rico. http://www.cie.uprp.edu

Bardhan I, Whitaker J, Mithas S (2006) Information technology, production process outsorcing and manufacturing plant performance. J Manage Inform Syst 23(2):13–40

Basem Hassan-Lombardi M (2012) La relación entre la inversión extranjera directa, el crecimiento económico, las exportaciones y el mercado laboral en Puerto Rico. Disertación doctoral, Universidad Interamericana de Puerto Rico

Basem Hassan-Lombardi M, Juma'h AH, Cue F, Ruiz Á, Llorens A (2012) La inversión extranjera directa, las exportaciones, el producto interno bruto y el mercado laboral en Puerto Rico. Ecos Econ 16(35):5–28

Basem-Hassan-Lombardi M, Juma'h AH (2014) Comparación macroeconómica entre Puerto Rico, Singapur e Irlanda utilizando un modelo de vectores autoregresivos. Rev Fin Pol Econ 6(1)

A.H. Juma'h et al., *Labor Markets and Multinational Enterprises in Puerto Rico*, SpringerBriefs in Economics, DOI 10.1007/978-3-319-17178-4

Blanco-Peck R (1992) El impacto de la cultura política dependiente de puerto rico. Rev Admin Públ 24(2):junio

Bram J, Martínez FE, Steindel C (2008) Tendencias y cambios en la economía de Puerto Rico. Fed Res Bank N Y 14(2):1–6

Broedner P, Kinkel S, Lay G (2009) Productivity effects of outsourcing-New evidence on the strategic importance of vertical integration decisions. Int J Oper Prod Manag 29:127–150

Business Monitor International (2006) Puerto Rico pharmaceuticals & healthcare report. www.mindbranch.com/Puerto-Rico-Pharmaceuticals-R302849/

Chang SC (2006) The dynamic interactions among foreign direct investment, economic growth, exports and unemployment: evidence from Taiwan. Econ Chang Restruct 38(3):235–256

Chang SC (2007) The interactions among foreign direct investment, economic growth, degree of openness and unemployment in Taiwan. Appl Econ 39(13):1647–1661

Chang DS, Kuo YC, Chen TY (2008) Productivity measurement of the manufacturing process for outsourcing decisions: the case of a Taiwanese printed circuit board manufacturer. Int J Prod Res 46:6981–6995

Chase RB, Aquilano NJ, Jacobs FR (1998) Productions and operations. Management-manufacturing and services. McGraw-Hill, New York, pp 470–471

Cheng LC (2007) Dynamics between contract manufacturing and operational performances: an empirical study of the U.S. manufacturing industries. POMS 18th annual conference, pp 1–27

CICAAE—Comité Intersectorial de Cumplimiento Ambiental y Alternativas Energéticas (2012) Informe Sobre las Medidas Necesarias para Cumplir con las Nuevas Reglas de la EPA, Conversión de Plantas y Uso de Gas Natural en las Plantas Generadoras del Norte, 15 June 2012

Christante de Mello L (2014) Publicación Científica en América Latina: posibilidades y oportunidades para los investigadores puertorriqueños. Workshop de Springer Publication in San Juan, Puerto Rico, Sept 2014

Collins SM, Bosworth BP, Soto-Class MA (2006) The economy of Puerto Rico: restoring growth. The Brookings Institution Press, Washington, DC

Custodio M (2010) Una fórmula llamada Daneris Fernández. El Nuevo Día, Negocios, 28 marzo 2010, p 8

Díaz-Mora C (2008) What factors determine the outsourcing intensity? A dynamic panel data approach for manufacturing industries. Appl Econ 40:2509–2521

Dietz JL (2001) Puerto Rico: Una economía de "tres pilares". http://www.iadb.org/intal/intalcdi/integracion_comercio/e_INTAL_IYC_15_2001_Dietz

Dietz JL (2003) Puerto Rico: negotiating development and change. Lynne Rienner Publishers, Inc., Boulder, CO

DLHR—Departamento del Trabajo y Recursos Humanos de Puerto Rico (1970) Serie Historia de Empleo y Desempleo en Puerto Rico de 1947–1969. Negociado de Estadísticas del Trabajo. http://www.estadisticas.gobierno.pr/iepr/LinkClick.aspx?fileticket=5wGH11-zY4w%3D&tabid=186

DLHR—Departamento del Trabajo y Recursos Humanos de Puerto Rico (2010) Serie Histórica de Empleo y Desempleo en Puerto Rico de 1970-2010. Negociado de Estadísticas del Trabajo. http//www.trabajo.pr.gov/pdf/Estadisticas/2013/GT/gtsh.pdf

DLHR—Departamento del Trabajo y Recursos Humanos de Puerto Rico (2013) Boletín de Empleo y Desempleo en Puerto Rico. Negociado de Estadísticas del Trabajo. http://www.trabajado.pr.gov/pdf/Estadisticas/2013/GT/gt7pdf. 19 de agosto de 2013

DLHR—Departamento del Trabajo y Recursos Humanos de Puerto Rico (2013) Empleo Asalariado No Agrícola. Negociado de Estadísticas del Trabajo. http//www.trabajo.pr.gov/Estadisticas/2013/CES/ces-8pdf. 20 de septiembre de 2013

DLHR—Departamento del Trabajo y Recursos Humanos de Puerto Rico (2014) Empleo Asalariado No Agrícola. Negociado de Estadísticas del Trabajo. http://www.trabajo.pr.gov/pdf/Estadisticas/2014/GT/gt08.pdf. 19 de septiembre de 2014

Dunning JH, Narula R (1995) The R&D activities of foreign firms in United States. Int Stud Manag Org 25(1–2):39–73

Ernest & Young (2010) Global pharmaceutical industry report. http://www.ey.com/...2010.../GPI_report_2010_Progressions_Pharma_3–1.pdf
Feenstra RC, Hanson GH (1996) Globalization, outsourcing, and wage inequality. Am Econ Rev 86:240–245
Girma S, Görg H (2004) Outsourcing, foreign ownership, and productivity: evidence from UK establishment-level data. Rev Int Econ 12:817–832
Gondor M, Nistor P (2012) Fiscal policy and foreign direct investment: evidence from some emerging EU economies. Proc Soc Behav Sci 58. http://www.sciencesdirect.com
Guajarati DN, Porter DC (2009) Basic econometrics, 5th edn. McGraw Hill, Singapur
Guillen M (2002) Structural inertia, imitation, and foreign expansion: South Korean Firms and Business Group in China 1987–1995. Acad Manage J 45(3)
Guillen N (2009) Las farmacéuticas y los medicamentos manufacturados en Puerto Rico. El Nuevo Día, 10 de febrero 2009
Hill CWL (2009) International business: competing in the global marketplace. Irwin, New York, p 194, 242, 342
ILO—Organización Internacional del Trabajo (2012) Panorama Laboral América Latina y el Caribe 2012. Oficina Regional de la OIT para América Latina y el Caribe. http://www.ilo.org/americas/publicaciones/WCMS_195884/lang--es/index.htm
INDUNIV-Research Consortium (2013) The life science industry. INDUNIV
International Monetary Fund (2011) World economic outlook database
Irizarry-Mora E (2000) Análisis sectorial de la economía de Puerto Rico. Ceterisparibus 2. http://ceterisparibus.uprm.edu/articulos/vol2/Analisis-sectorial.htm
Jiang B, Frazier GV, Prater EL (2006) Outsourcing effects on firms' operational performance: an empirical study. Int J Oper Prod Manag 26:1280–1300
Jiang B, Belohlav JA, Young ST (2007) Outsourcing impact on manufacturing firms' value: evidence from Japan. JOper Manag 25:885–900
Johansen S, Juselius K (1990) Maximum likelihood estimation and inference on cointegration – with applications to the demand for money. Oxford Bull Econ Stat 52(2):169–210
Juma'h AH, Wood D (1999) Outsourcing implications for accounting practices. Manag Audit J 14:387–395
Juma'h AH, Wood D (2000) Outsourcing implications on companies profitability and liquidity a sample of UK companies. Work Stud 49:265–274
Kliksberg B, Rivera M (2007) El Capital Social Movilizado Contra la Pobreza: La Experiencia del Proyecto de Comunidades Especiales en Puerto Rico. Consejo Latinoamericano de Ciencias Sociales, Organización de las Naciones Unidas. Buenos Aires, diciembre de 2007. ISBN 978-987-1183-80-7. http://www.clacso.org.ar/libreria-latinoamericana/libro_detalle.php?id_libro=81&pageNum_rs_libros=46&totalRows_rs_libros=788
Laboy J, Toledo W (2006) Los determinantes de la supervivencia de las empresas de manufactura en una economía pequeña y abierta: El caso de Puerto Rico. http://www.cepal.org/ilpes/noticias/paginas/.../laboytoledo_final_CEPAL.org
Landaru-Febres A (2013) La Relación entre la Subcontratación (Outsourcing) del Sector Manufacturero de Puerto Rico con Factores Financieros y Económicos. Disertación doctoral, Universidad Interamericana de Puerto Rico
Lipsey RE, Swedenborg B (2007) Explaining product price differences across countries. National Bureau of Economic Research, Cambridge, MA, pp 1–40
Marin D (2006) A new international division of labor in Europe: outsourcing and offshoring to Eastern Europe. J Eur Econ Assoc 4:612–622
Martínez JM, Máttar J, Rivera P (2004) Globalización y desarrollo: Desafíos de Puerto Rico frente al siglo XXI. Comisión Económica para América Latina y el Caribe (CEPAL), México, DF
Marxuach SM (2012) Despoblación. Perspectivas, año XIX, vol VII. Estudios Técnicos, Inc., Puerto Rico
Mohiuddin M, Su Z, Su A (2010) Towards sustainable offshore outsourcing: a case study of Quebec manufacturing firms outsourcing to China. J CENTRUM Cathedra 3(1):84–94

Morales D, Juma'h A, Llorens-Rivera A Cue F, Ruiz A (2012) Tendencias del traslado de actividades en las manufactureras en Puerto Rico y el título de propiedad sobre la planta física, 2005–2011. Atlant Rev Econ 2

Morales-Rodríguez D (2012) Determinantes en el Traslado de Operaciones de las Multinacionales Establecidas en Puerto Rico; Una Muestra en el Sector Manufactura 2005–2011. Disertación doctoral, Universidad Interamericana de Puerto Rico

New York FED—Federal Reserve Bank of New York (2012) Informe sobre la competitividad de la economía de Puerto Rico. http://www.newyorkfed.org/regional/puertorico/spanish.html

OECD—Organisation For Economic Cooperation and Development (2008) Annual report. http://www.oecd.org/newsroom/40556222pdf

Paul DL, Wooster RB (2010) An empirical analysis of motives for offshore outsourcing by U.S. firms. Int Trade J 24(3):298–320

Percival J, Cozzarin B (2010) Selecting manufacturing business practices for maximum competitive advantage. J Manuf Technol Manag 21:100–121

Pfaff B (2008) Analysis of integrated and cointegrated time series with R. Springer, Washington, DC

Pharmaceutical Research and Manufacturers of America (PhRMA) (2011) Pharmaceutical industry profile 2011. PhRMA, Washington, DC

PIA—Pharmaceutical Industry Asociation of Puerto Rico (2011) Industrial incentive. http://www.piapr.org/index.php?submenu=Indicentives&src=gendocs&ref=IndustrialIncentives&category=Main

PIE—Pharmaceutical Industry Executives (2013) Presentación del Grupo PIE Ante la Trigésima Asamblea Anual de la Asociación de Economistas de Puerto Rico. Presentación provista por PIE

Pindyck RS, Rubinfeld DI (1991) Econometric models & economic forecast. Mc Graw-Hill, New York

Planning Board—Junta de Planificación (1982–1983) Apéndice Estadístico. Informe Económico al Gobernador. San Juan, Puerto Rico

Plannning Board—Junta de Planificación (1990) Apéndice Estadístico. Informe Económico al Gobernador. San Juan, Puerto Rico

Planning Board—Junta de Planificación (2000). Apéndice Estadístico. Informe Económico al Gobernador. San Juan, Puerto Rico

Planning Board—Junta de Planificación (2010) Apéndice Estadístico. Informe Económico al Gobernador. San Juan, Puerto Rico

Planning Board—Junta de Planificación (2012) Revisión de series de empleo y series ajustadas estacionalmente. "Indicadores Económicos", en "Actividad Económica". http://www.jp.gobierno.pr/

Planning Board—Junta de Planificación (2013) Estadísticas Macroeconómicas. Tabla 23 – Exportaciones de mercancía registrada por sistema de clasificación industrial de América del Norte (SCIAN): Años Fiscales. http://www.jp.gobierno.pr/Portal_JP/Portals/0/ApendiceEstadistico/AE%20T–23.pdf

Pol J (2004) Determinantes económicos de la migración en Puerto rico y Estado Unidos. Ensayo 119, Unidad de Investigaciones Económicas, Departamento de Economía, Universidad de Puerto Rico. http://economia.uprrp.edu/ensayo%20119.pdf

PRIDCO—Compañía de Fomento Industrial de Puerto Rico (2006) Reglamento para la Administración de Incentivos para las Industrias en Puerto Rico, según enmendado (MO-INC-001) 7125. Departamento de Estado de Puerto Rico, Núm. Reglamento 7250

PRIDCO—Compañía de Fomento Industrial de Puerto Rico (2009) Reglamento para la Administración del Fondo Especial para el Desarrollo Económico (MODNE-002). Departamento de Estado de Puerto Rico, Núm. Reglamento 7736

Rezitis AN, Kalantzi MA (2011) Investigating market structure of the Greek manufacturing industry: a Hall-Roeger approach. Atlant Econ J 39:383–400

Rodríguez C, Bustillo R (2010) Un análisis de los procesos de deslocalización productiva: inversión extranjera directa e importación de bienes intermedios en la Industria Vasca. Cuadernos de Relaciones Laborales 28(1)

Rodríguez CA (2002) Análisis dinámico de la economía de Puerto Rico con un modelo de vectores autorregresivos y cointegración. Series de Ensayos y Monografías. Unidad de Investigaciones Económicas, Universidad de Puerto Rico (110), pp 1–16
Rodríguez CA (2004) Conceptos básicos y aspectos matemáticos sobre el análisis de raíces unitarias y cointegración. Ceteris Paribus 4(9):1–30
Rodríguez CA (2008) La evolución histórica, la teoría económica y el sistema económico deseable como bases fundamentales para desarrollar una estrategia de desarrollo económico en Puerto Rico. Serie de Ensayos y Monografías. Unidad de Investigaciones Económicas, Universidad de Puerto Rico (136). http://economia.uprrp.edu/ensayo%20carlos%rodriguez.pdf
Ruiz A (2006) Cambios en los niveles de productividad por sector industrial en la economía de Puerto Rico: 1963–2003. Revista Empresarial Inter Metro (Spring) 2(1)
Ruiz A (2007) La relación de la industria de servicios con la manufactura. Serie de Ensayos y Monografías. Unidad de Investigaciones Económicas, Universidad de Puerto Rico (132). http://economia.uprpr.edu/ensayo%20132-Angel%Ruiz.pdf
Schilling MA, Steensma HK (2001) The use of modular organizational forms: an industry-level analysis. Acad Manage J 44(6):1149–1168
Schniederjans MJ, Zuckweiler KM (2004) A quantitative approach to the outsourcing-insourcing decision in an international context. Manag Decis 42:974–986
Sen S, Zhu G (1996) The optimal degree of outsourcing. J Fin Strateg Decis 9:63–70
Silva-Huyke A (2013) Pertinencia del Enfoque de Desarrollo Económico Local para la Realidad Puertorriqueña. Presentado en la Trigésima Conferencia Anual de la Asociación de Economistas, Utilizando Nuestros Recursos para Promover el Desarrollo, 30 de agosto de 2013
Sims CA (1980) Macroeconomics and reality. Econometrica 48(1):1–46
The World Economic Forum (2012) The global competitiveness report 2012–2013. K. Schwab, Geneva
The World Economic Forum (2013) The global competitiveness report 2013–2014. K. Schwab, Geneva
Toledo W (2009) Los impactos de impulsos agregados y sectoriales sobre la trayectoria del empleo en Puerto Rico. Ensayo 146, Unidad de Investigaciones Económicas, Departamento de Economía, Universidad de Puerto Rico. http://economia.uprrp.edu/toledoEnsayo 146.pdf
Tomiura E, Ito B, Wakasugi R (2011) Offshore outsourcing decision and capital intensity: firm-level relationships. Econ Inq 49(2):364–378
Torres-Morales T (2013) Estudio sobre los determinantes para el establecimiento de centros de R&D: Caso de las farmacéuticas en Puerto Rico. Disertación doctoral, Universidad Interamericana, Puerto Rico
United Nations (2011) UNCTAD STAT
United Nations (2012) UNCTAD STAT
U.S. Census Bureau (2005) Puerto Rico manufacturing 2002 economic census of island areas, pp 1–105. http://www.census.gov
U.S. Census Bureau (2011) Puerto Rico manufacturing 2007 economic census of island areas. http://www.census.gov/econ/islandareas/new_historical.html
U.S. Department of Labor (2011) Bureau of labor statistics, local area unemployment statistics (LAUS)
Villamil JJ (2012) Demografía y Desarrollo Económico. Perspectivas, año XIX, núm VII. Estudios Técnicos, Inc., Puerto Rico
Yeaple SR (2006) Offshoring, foreign direct investment and the structure of US trade. J Eur Econ Assoc 4(2–3):602–611

MIX
Papier aus verantwortungsvollen Quellen
Paper from responsible sources
FSC® C105338

If you have any concerns about our products,
you can contact us on
ProductSafety@springernature.com

In case Publisher is established outside the EU,
the EU authorized representative is:
Springer Nature Customer Service Center GmbH
Europaplatz 3, 69115 Heidelberg, Germany

Printed by Libri Plureos GmbH
in Hamburg, Germany